C PROGRAMMING WITH BUSINESS APPLICATIONS

C PROGRAMMING WITH BUSINESS APPLICATIONS

DR. LEON A. WORTMAN AND
THOMAS O. SIDEBOTTOM

TAB BOOKS Inc.
Blue Ridge Summit, PA 17214

FIRST EDITION
FIRST PRINTING

Library of Congress Cataloging in Publication Data

Wortman, Leon A.
C programming—with business applications.

Includes index.
1. C (Computer program language) 2. Business—Data processing. I. Sidebottom, Thomas O., 1956- . II. Title.
HF5548.5.C12W67 1987 005.2'65 86-23090
ISBN 0-8306-1457-5
ISBN 0-8306-2857-6 (pbk.)

Contents

Acknowledgments

We sincerely acknowledge and appreciate the outstanding work being done by software authors and publishers who have developed and continue to improve their C compilers. Where would we be without their pioneering efforts? We thank them for the opportunities they offer to those of us who want to grow and advance as C programmers.

Our thanks are given to the editorial staff of TAB BOOKS, Inc., publisher of this book, for their recognition of the growing interest in C as a vital and dynamic language for useful applications programs. Also, our sincere gratitude is expressed to Dr. Mark Scott Johnston for his professional critiques of the source code, and to Dorothy F. Wortman for her dedicated work in coordinating our communications with the editors and the production group at TAB BOOKS Inc., and in coping with the complex logistics of putting together a book from the idea stage to the final printed copy.

And certainly, we thank you, the reader, for supporting our efforts.

Thomas O. Sidebottom
Leon A. Wortman
Palo Alto, California

Introduction: Something Very Special

This book is "something very special." It is chock-full of programs written entirely in the C programming language. The programs are useful applications programs and will be especially valuable and appealing to those who get a kick out of hacking at somebody else's code. Be our guest!

This book is not intended to serve as a primary tutorial for those who want to learn C programming from the ground up. There are other books dedicated to that process, but most of them are deficient in the amount of program code with which the reader may practice. We tried to be different, *better* in that respect, believing that there is more than one way to teach and to learn a programming language. This book approaches the learning/teaching process in a relatively unstructured way. You will learn by doing: by entering code in the C programming language, by working with the code, by modifying it and revising it. In this way you can try, test, observe, experience, and increase your knowledge of the practice as well as the theory of programming in C.

A good measure of tutorial materials has been provided. Each program's source code listing includes comments—brief explanations of the purpose of the code. In this way, important tutorial elements not specifically included in the text have been placed as comments in the code listings where they rightfully belong. It is important to read the comments carefully.

Working with somebody else's code, experimenting with the changes in a bit of source code here and another bit there to see what effects the changes have on the program, is an excellent way to learn a programming language. Through this means and method many people have learned or have become self-taught and skilled with programming languages.

Putting theory into practice, this book offers tools and programs that are valuable and useful to anyone—novice or veteran, student or professional—interested in learning or advancing his or her knowledge of the exciting C programming language.

In addition to the intellectual exercises and the valuable and enjoyable experience you can gain, one of the nice things about these programs is that they run and will perform useful work. Some of the programs are for use in business. Others are suited for the reader's personal affairs. All contain sections of code and functions you may find adaptable to your original programs and needs.

Every professional, and probably many experienced nonprofessional programmers, builds sets of files of routines that can be included in source code for programs and utilities. This is a time-saving method. After all, why reinvent the wheel each time you go for a ride? It's plainly prudent to use or adapt the routines offered in this book. They're ready to run—tested and debugged.

Complete source code is provided for each of the programs in Chapters 1 through 29. Descriptions of the utility of the programs are furnished in each chapter to help you understand each program's usefulness. Where they are useful in learning C, sample runs are included to show the results produced by the programs.

Each program's code is commented—a means for providing you with tutorial information as well as an exceptionally effective means to help you learn as you go.

As we explore the terrain of the C programming language, we feel some of the excitement, the joy of discovery that early travelers and land pioneers must have felt. This isn't intended as corny sentiment. The C programming language is filled with new challenges; those who will accept these challenges and participate in the journeys will also share in rich intellectual rewards.

The C programming language is young, still in its formative years. If you do not obey the rules of its syntax, it can be as sensitive and unforgiving as a new frontier can be. The similarities and compatibilities of code written in C can be defeated by the differences in the runtime libraries supplied with commercially available compilers. One compiler may readily (or with a few "warnings") accept code and generate an executable file. Another compiler may stubbornly refuse to deal with the same code, rejecting it totally. Don't fault the code; study the documentation supplied with the compiler. Search for what appear to be idiosyncrasies related to the requirements of the run-time library used in processing the code, make the required changes in the source code, and try the compiling and linking processes again.

Although there may be valid, technical reasons for individual preferences among programmers, compilers are subjective things—either you like them or you don't. Some you may prefer to avoid. You may feel more comfortable with others. You may prefer one compiler for a certain type of application, another for other applications. "Why I like the XYZ-Compiler" is a favorite topic discussion (bordering on the dedication of religious devotees) when professional programmers get together. All arguments have validity.

A shortcoming of many books of source code is that they neglect or forget to name the compiler used to test and debug the code. This book is a reflection of our primary preference for a compiler written to run on the IBM PC series. Our choice for the compiler for the programs in this book is Microsoft C, Version 4.0, published by the Microsoft Corporation. Why? Simply because the Microsoft C library and UNIX System V are compatible.

The programs in this book can be compiled with all versions of the Microsoft C compiler. We enjoy working with Microsoft, whose customer support is competent and cooperative. No doubt other manufacturers are equally acceptable, but keeping costs and time in mind, how can one try them all?

Our preference shouldn't rule out the genuine values offered by other compilers. If you enjoy and prefer to use the "foobah" compiler and with it obtain the desired results, then that's a fine compiler for you. More power and joy to you!

The description of compilers often includes the phrase "follows the K&R (Kernighan & Ritchie) standard." This is inadequate and possibly is misleading. While all C compilers have great similarities and even support the same language syntax, there are differences in the built-in functions in their libraries. The differences may make one compiler refuse to accept the code of a particular program while another compiler may have no trouble at all.

Again, we emphasize that the compiler used in testing and processing the source code given in this book is Microsoft C, Version 4.0. Appendices A and B contain source code for the utilities used in each chapter in this book. Appendix C provides instructions on how to create batch files for the IBM PC, IBM XT, IBM AT, and compatible computers. These virtually automate the compiling and linking processes.

The source code in these pages may compile and execute only with other compilers. However, it isn't practical to list all the variations for the growing number of compilers being marketed, nor has it been practicable for us to test all of the compilers that are available for use with microcomputers.

If you are not using the Microsoft C compiler, and if the code doesn't compile without errors or doesn't produce executable files, we urge you to check your compiler's error messages and documentation for the correct use of its library functions. The statement that the compiler "is K&R compatible" is not a guarantee the compiler will work with all source code that is "K&R compatible." Check for differences or uniqueness in your compiler's library; make the appropriate alterations in syntax to suit the requirements of your compiler.

We assume you've entered the source code correctly with whatever happens to be your favorite text editor. (If you don't like all that typing, you can obtain the source code for each of the programs in this book already entered on a disk in the IBM-PC format. Ordering information is given at the end of this book.)

The C language lets us create and assign original names to individual functions, groups or sections of code. To provide good comprehension of each of the functions, we have chosen names that help identify the functions' purposes. You may rename them to suit your own needs for mnemonic devices.

While popular emphasis is on IBM-compatible microcomputers, the source code in this book is well suited to a myriad of computers. C is not hardware-dependent; although C compilers are dependent upon the operating system, this book's programs have been written to be hardware independent. With modifications in syntax when required, according to the documentation for the particular compiler you prefer to use, the programs may compile and execute under virtually any operating system and microcomputer hardware for which a C code compiler is available.

This is a book of source code for applications programs written in the C programming language. The programs are not intended to replace or substitute for the "fully developed" commercially-available software packages. They are for the purpose of providing a learning experience to those who will study the form and substance of the sets of code and the actions they generate. We have endeavored to supply tutorials with each of the programs, some of which is given in the text that precedes each program, some included as comments in each program's code. We believe we have found a novel presentation for tutorial materials in Chapter 3.

Here are a few items of interest for book-production technologists. The manuscript was produced with NewWord3 (NewStar Software, Inc). The source code was developed with the VEDIT editor (CompuView Products, Inc). The integrity of the programs was tested with the Microsoft C Compiler, Versions 3.0 and 4.0 (Microsoft Corporation). Printouts of the manuscript were made with a Hewlett Packard LaserJet; text for the editorial and production staffs of TAB BOOKS Inc. was printed with the internal Courier-10 font. The text was then edited, set in galleys from the word-processing disks, and converted to page mechanicals for production printing. The source code for all programs was printed on the Hewlett Packard LaserJet with the Prestige Elite font cartridge. These printouts were used as camera-ready artwork for printing the listings. The sample runs of the code were prepared with a Fujitsu DPL24I dot-matrix printer; these, too, were used as camera-ready artwork.

What you see is what we got!

1

It's Fundamental

Every tutorial in programming must have a beginning. We all want to learn rapidly, so this chapter will help you get off to a fast start, a clear beginning. We'll write a simple program that will demonstrate the first essentials in writing code in the C programming language. Using your favorite text editor, or your word processor in the non-formatted editing mode, enter the lines of code in Fig. 1-1.

To save the code to disk, your editor or word processor requires you to name the file. You may give it any name that is legal under the disk operating system. The first line in the example gives it the name Prog1.c. This is an arbitrary choice, not a requirement of the C programming language. However, the letter or extension "c" following the file's name *is* a requirement. To avoid confusion, if you use another name make the appropriate change in the first line; and don't forget the ".c" extension.

The first line of the example begins with a backslash followed immediately by an asterisk. The line ends with the same two characters, but in reverse order. These characters signal the compiler that any text between the two pairs (backslash-asterisk and asterisk-backslash) are comments for human reading only. The compiler ignores these pairs of symbols and anything in-between them. If they are not paired the compiler will refuse to accept the code and probably display an error message on the video screen; likewise, if you insert a space between the backslashes and the asterisks. We have also entered comments after the left-facing and the right-facing braces.

The line beginning with the expression **printf** tells the executable pro-

Fig. 1-1. Program 1—we write our first program in C.

```
/* This is my first program in C. I shall call it "Progl.c" */

main()
{       /* begin the main function */
        printf("If I can read this,\nProgl works!") ;
}       /* end the main function */
```

gram to display the characters enclosed in the quotation marks and surrounded by the paired left and right parentheses. So, **printf** means we want to display something, to send it to the video console. The "something" is surrounded by matching pairs of parentheses and double quotation marks. The matching of these characters is essential; they come only in pairs. The compiler will insist on it.

Go back to the first line in the example. The C programming language is very structured. An executable program is composed of groups of functions. The minimum number of functions is one. And that single function is always labelled **main.** No matter how many functions your program has, it must include a main function. Function names are followed by a paired set of parentheses, as shown in Fig. 1-1. Function names may contain a combination of characters and digits, but no punctuation marks. The name must be a continuous string of characters.

The underscore is recognized as a character. It is often used in the name of a function or a variable to enhance the human reader's ability to make sense out of the names we contrive for functions. For example, to use the combination of words "get the facts" as a function name with its own mnemonic, we could type it as: Get_The_Facts. The compiler's requirement for one-word names for functions is satisfied, as in the human need for separations between words.

The left brace following **main()** indicates that the contents of the function begin at that point. The right brace indicates end of the main function, as the comments tell us.

Try entering, saving, compiling, and running Prog1 (or whatever you've named it). If you've written the code exactly as above and have followed the proper procedure for compiling it, a check of your disk's directory will show that a new file has been generated: prog1.exe. Execute the file by typing the program's name and you will see the **printf** message displayed flush left on the video screen:

If I can read this,
Prog1 works!

What's this? We entered the code on one line but it displayed on two lines! Notice the forward slash followed immediately by the letter n. This pair, **\n**, when included in the string of characters enclosed by the paired parentheses and the double quotation marks, is referred to as a "newline," equivalent to a carriage return. Placing it where we did broke the line after the comma and placed the rest of the string on the next (new) line.

The compiler ignores visible line breaks. It compiles everything as though it were a continuous one-line string. We add the spaces and put expressions on separate lines to help us understand the code better when we read it. We could have entered the code this way:

```
main( ) { /* begin the main function */ printf("If I can read this,
Prog1 works!") ; } /* end the main function */
```

It would make no difference to the compiler, but it is certainly more difficult for human reading. Imagine trying to comprehend and analyze code, even your own code, written as a continuous stream. So, we've created this convention for our own benefit. However, inside a pair of double quotation marks, which enclose a literal string of characters or words, the spacing must be typed following each separate word and its related punctuation mark.

Common practice is to type the names of functions in lowercase. Or, if you prefer it for clarity, enter the first character of a function's name in uppercase. You will rarely, if ever, see **main()** in other than lowercase characters—usually **main()** must be typed in lowercase.

If you choose to ignore our advice, try experimenting with a variety of combinations of upper- and lowercase characters for the **main** and **printf** functions in the example. Compile the code with these changes and see for yourself whether the compiler accepts them. The expression **main()** is conventionally entered in the first column, the flush-left margin of the file. This is not mandatory for **main()** but we will soon see that it is absolutely required when certain other expressions are typed in as part of the code.

A semicolon is required to signal the end of a statement. The **printf** expression is a *function.* It begins and ends with a matching pair of parentheses. This, plus the characters enclosed by the double quotation marks, form a complete *statement* in the C programming language. Therefore, the semicolon is used to terminate the statement.

Those are the barest fundamentals of the C programming language. There's much more to it, much more power. Complexity seems to come with power. To give you a mild flavor of the increasing intricacies and power, in the next chapter we'll whet our appetites by building more interesting capability into the simplicity of Prog1. Then we'll go on into a wide variety of applications programs and commented source code, all intended to enhance your knowledge and enjoyment of C.

2

It Gets More Interesting

Let's repeat the code for Prog1.c and do some work on it, add to its power. We'll name the revised version **Prog2.c**. Refer to Fig. 1-1 in Chapter 1 when necessary.

We'll start the code with a call to another file we want to include in the program. Almost all C programs begin with a call to the standard input-output file **stdio.h**. It is supplied as part of the compiler. Be aware that two inflexible rules of C are that the "include" expression must be preceded by the pound sign (#) with absolutely no intervening space between that sign and the word include, and the # sign must be at the flush left margin on the screen, in column 1.

Aside from comments and the program name, **#include** calls are entered before anything else, including the **main( )** expression. The file being called is usually placed between a matching pair of left and right arrows. For example, we could have started Prog1.c with the line:

```
#include <stdio.h>
```

Our simple example, Prog1.c, compiles and runs without the **#include** call to **stdio.h** because we merely wanted to display a message on the screen. Because screen display is the normal default condition for directing **printf** commands, **#include <stdio.h>** was not necessary. In many of the examples in this book we will see how we can direct the output of a program to the printer or to create a file on the disk. It is important to enter this line; make it a habit to do so. From here on you will see it in each of the programs in this book.

ENHANCING Prog1.c

For now let's modify the code to make the program ask us a question, wait for our response, and then display our answer. Enter and compile the code in Fig. 2-1. Notice the variations we've included in the code, some of which are intended only to affect the appearance of the output. The newline (carriage return) directive, **\n**, can be placed virtually anywhere within a string of literal characters surrounded by double quotation marks. It can be put at the start as well as at the end of a string—wherever we want the program to execute a carriage return.

There are a series of commands referred to as "escaped characters" which are identical in construction to the newline character you are familiar with: the sequence of a backslash followed by certain single letters or punctuation marks. They are specifically recognized by the compiler and behave as a shorthand instruction in a program. Table 2-1 is a list of those that are most commonly used by programmers.

We could have used any word or combination of characters our compiler would accept, but we are going to use **Number** to carry the assignment of the value we give to our response to the question following the first **printf.** We will use an integer value, a whole number. At the beginning, right after the left brace following **main( )** we enter the identification **int Number**, which directs the compiler to interpret the values assigned to **Number** as whole numbers—not fractions, decimals, floating, or exponentials.

Whereas **printf** *displays* characters, **scanf** *gets* characters. **printf** is for output, **scanf** is for input. The symbol **%d** follows through on the fact that

Fig. 2-1. Program 2—an interactive version of Program 1.

```
/* This is my second program in C. I shall name it "Prog2.c" */

#include <stdio.h>

main()
{    /* begin the main function */

        int Number ;  /* identify the word Number as an integer */

        printf("\nWhat is the number of the chapter you are reading? ") ;
        scanf("%d",&Number) ;

        printf("You typed the number %d\n\n",Number) ;
        printf("If you can read this line, Prog2 works!\n") ;

 }    /* end the main function */
```

CHARACTER	USAGE
\n	newline
\r	carriage return
\b	backspace
\t	horizontal tab
\v	vertical tab
\f	form feed
\\	backslash character
\"	double quotation mark
\'	single quotation mark

Table 2-1. Partial List of "Backslash" Operators.

Number is to be an integer value. An ampersand must precede the identifier (**Number**, in this case) when it is used with **scanf**.

We've spaced the lines of code to make them easier for human reading. This makes no difference to the compiler.

ENHANCING Prog2.c

Let's carry on further with our fundamental source code for Prog2.c. Suppose we want to make certain the program continues with the proper action only when the user enters the correct response to the request for the number of the chapter you are reading—this chapter, which is 2. In fact, we can rewrite the code so that it tells the user an incorrect answer was entered, and persistently repeats the request until the correct answer is entered. That's what we have in Fig. 2-2, which we call "Prog3." You will frequently see its construction in the programs in this book. The code for Prog3 is commented to explain its operations.

The chapters that follow are dedicated to a collection of programs that contain a variety of examples of the structure, power, and flexibility of C.

Table 2-2 lists many of the special characters, operators and symbols that are an important part of the syntax of C. Learn them and memorize or keep them close at hand. They will help you comprehend the combinations of alphanumerics and punctuation marks that characterize C.

While many C programming language expressions are written with familiar words, others appear to be abbreviations, contractions or something akin to acronyms. Some cannot be easily verbalized; they have to be spelled rather than pronounced, or may combine spelling and pronunciation. (For example, **fprintf** is pronounced eff-print-eff, **fputs** becomes eff-put-ess, **getc** is expressed as get-see.) Although we've never tried to had the skill to do so, we're willing to believe that attempting to speak fluently in C might be similar to speaking in the language of hieroglyphics. It's easier to write than speak it.

The code for the programs in the chapters that follow makes use of much of the "shorthand" or special constructions of the professional person who regularly programs in the C language. We may frequently repeat ourselves, using and reusing some of the comments included in the code. (You recall: comments begin with /* and end with */; always in matching pairs.) Our intent is to rein-

Fig. 2-2. Program 3—an exercise in error-trapping.

```
/* This is my third program in C. I shall name it "Prog3.c" */

/* Include files
*/
#include <stdio.h>

main() {                          /* begin the main function */

    int     Number;               /* declare Number as an integer */

    printf("\nWhat is the number of the chapter you are reading? ");
    scanf("%d", &Number);

/* Trap wrong Number entries larger or smaller than 2; accept
   only the correct Number.  Use a "while" loop to test whether
   the number entered was not equal (!=) to 2.  If the Number
   entered is the integer 2, jump out of the loop, pass the right
   curly bracket, and continue. */
    while (Number != 2) {

/* If the number was > or < 2, display the error message and
   the number that was actually entered. */
        printf("\nYou typed the number %d and that's wrong.", Number);

/* And repeat the question. */
        printf("\nAgain, what is the number of the chapter you are reading? ");
        scanf("%d", &Number);
    }

/* We are now outside the loop and continuing the program. */
    printf("\nGreat! Prog3 and the error trap work ok!\n");

}                                 /* end the main function */
```

force the learning experience without detracting from the pleasure derived from working with code.

Table 2-2. A Table of C Operators and Symbols.

Operator/ Symbol	Function	Operator/ Symbol	Function	Operator/ Symbol	Function
+	addition	/=	divide and assign	||	logical OR
-	subtraction	==	equal to	&&	logical AND
*	multiplication	<	less than	!=	not equal to
/	division	<=	less than or equal to	%	modulus
++	increment	=<	less than or equal to	%c	display a character
--	decrement	>	greater than	%d	display an integer value
=	assignment	=>	greater than or equal to	%e	display an exponential notation
+=	add and assign	>=	greater than or equal to	%f	display a float value
-=	subtract and assign	{	begin a group of statements	%s	display a string of characters
*=	multiply and assign	}	end a group of statements	<>	a compiler directive

3

Parts of the C Program

The primary purpose of this book is to give you a collection of C programs that can be compiled and executed. Rather than read through descriptions of how the C language works, you have the opportunity to learn C by reading real programs and experimenting with them. You need a reading knowledge of C, though, to use the book. This chapter provides diagrams that set out the fundamentals of C. By looking through the figures and reading the accompanying text you will learn enough about C to be able to read and comprehend the programs.

IDENTIFIERS AND DECLARATIONS

An *identifier* is a name you use to reference elements inside a program. Table 3-1 describes the identifiers C accepts. Identifiers always begin with a letter and continue with letters and digits. For most systems identifiers are case-sensitive, and they are unique to the first thirty-one characters.

A *declaration* is the way you create a variable inside a program. A variable is actually a place in memory that stores information. C programs operate on variables, transforming them into new values that have important meaning.

All variables in C are declared before use. A declaration associates an identifier-name with the kind of data that can be stored there. Table 3-2 details the different kinds of data that C programs can use. Table 3-3 describes what declarations look like.

Table 3-1.

Identifiers	
An identifier is a name you make up to identify elements of your program. The name should be meaningful to you.	
Start with a letter	Uppercase A through Z Lowercase a through z Underscore is a letter
Continue with letters and digits	Any letter above, plus any digit 0 through 9
Unique to 31 characters	
Case-sensitive	ABC is not the same identifier as abc.
Good identifiers	Valhalla, river, _index
Bad identifiers	0abc BC$* TU9(

OPERATORS

An *operator* is the symbol in a programming language for a basic function like addition or subtraction. C has many operators. It uses symbolic operators where other languages use words, and it uses operators for functions that do not exist in other languages. Table 3-4 lists the various kinds of operators that C has.

Table 3-5 describes the basic arithmetic operators in C. Unlike many lan-

Table 3-2.

Declarations

You describe the way you want to store data in your program using declarations. A declaration associates an identifier that you create with a kind of storage.

Standard Types

A variable's type describes what kind of data you want to store in it. It defines the size of the variable. C provides a number of standard types for storing data.

char	For storing characters. On most machines, a char is eight bits long.
short	For storing small numbers. On many machines, a short can store a number between -128 and 127
int	For storing integers. On many machines, an int can store a number between -32768 and 32767
long	For storing large integers. On many machines, a long can store a number as large as four billion.
float	For storing floating point numbers.
double	For storing extended precision floating point numbers.

guages, C has no exponentiation operator.

In complex arithmetic expressions with several operators, C uses rules to determine which operator to execute first. These rules are called *precedence rules,* and Table 3-6 details these rules.

One of the most fundamental operations in any language is taking the result of a computation and assigning it to a location in memory. Table 3-7 shows C's *assignment operator.* C uses special jargon to refer to the right and left hand sides of an assignment, Table 3-8. The right-hand side of an assignment is

Table 3-3.

Writing Declarations

Format	type identifier_name ;
Use the C standard type name to begin the declaration.	
Follow the type with the identifier you want to declare.	
End the declaration with a semicolon	
Examples	char Response ; int Counter ; double Average ;
Declarating many variables	You may declare many variables of the same type by listing all the identifier names after the type, separating them with commas.
Examples	char Value, Response, CorrectResponse ; int Counter, Index ;

called an r-val. R-vals are the result of computation. The left-hand side of an assignment is an l-val ("l" is lowercase L); these are variables where the result of computations may be placed.

C's *relational operators* appear in Table 3-9. Relational operators let the program test two values using a specified comparison test. Relational operators may be combined into more complex tests using logical operators, described in Table 3-10.

C provides operators which are shorthand ways of writing common expressions. Table 3-11 shows the *increment and decrement operators*; these oper-

Table 3-4.

Operators	
Operators are the symbols you use in a program to work with your data. C has a wide variety of operators.	
Arithmetic operators	Perform basic arithmetic
Assignment operator	Assign results of computations to variables
Relational operators	Compare variable values
Logical operators	Combine simple comparisons into complex logical tests
Increment operators	Increment or decrement a variable's value
Combined operators	Perform arithmetic and assign the value in a single step
Pointer operators **Specialized operators**	Advanced operators we will discuss later

ators either add or subtract one from a variable. Increment and decrement are such common tasks that these operators are used very frequently in C programs.

Often a program takes a variable, adds a quantity to it, and stores it again in the same variable. C combines *arithmetic and assignment operators,* shown in Table 3-12, to perform these tasks neatly.

STATEMENTS AND CONTROL STRUCTURES

The *statement* is the basic unit of program action. While declarations define variables, statements define an action for the program to perform. Statements in C are either expressions involving operators or one of the special statements described below. Statements in C end with a semicolon. Table 3-13 discusses these points.

Table 3-5.

Arithmetic Operators

Operator	Description
+	Add two numbers together
-	Subtract the second number from the first
*	Multiply two numbers together
/	Divide the first number by the second, and keep the quotient
%	Divide the first number by the second, and keep the remainder (modulus operator)

All these operators work with any numeric data type (short, int, long, float,double), except for the modulus operator, which works with integer data types only (short, int, long). C also lets you treat character data (char type) as a number.

Conditional Control: The If-Else Construction

Programs make decisions based on the result of tests. C's *if statement*, shown in Table 3-14, is the way C programs make simple tests. If the test is true, the statement following the **if** is executed. Table 3-15 shows how *multiple statements* enclosed in braces become a *compound statement* that an if statement can control.

Sometimes the program must take action if a test is false. C's *else statement*, Table 3-16, shows a way to control this case.

Loops

C gives several kinds of *loop structures* to repeatedly execute a section of code. Table 3-17 shows the *while loop*. This loop tests a condition before running the statements inside the loop. After all loop statements run, the test is made again. The loop continues to execute until the test fails.

Table 3-6.

Arithmetic Operator Precedence

If you combine several operators in a single expression, there may be many different ways to evaluate the expression, depending on the order the operators are evaluated.

Precedence defines the order of evaluation of operators.

For arithmetic operators:

- **Do all multiplication and division first, moving left to right through the expression.**
- **Do addition and subtraction next, moving left to right through the expression.**

To alter the order of evaluation:

- **Put the section to evaluate first inside parentheses.**

Examples

Value + Time * Seconds	multiply Time and Seconds first, then add Value
(Value + Time) * Seconds	add Value and Time first, then multiply by Seconds

The *do-while* loop in Table 3-18 is similar to the while loop, but the test appears at the bottom of the loop. The body of the loop always executes at least once.

The *for loop,* shown in Table 3-19 is the most complex of C's looping constructions. The *for loop* is shorthand for a *while loop,* as the figure shows.

Many times a program must stop running a loop. Rather than require use of a *goto* statement, as many languages do, C provides the *break statement*, Ta-

Table 3-7.

Assignment Operator

The assignment operator lets you place the result of a calculation into a variable.

Target = Response + 15 + A / B

- Target: Where the result will go
- =: The assigment operator
- Response + 15 + A / B: The expression to evaluate: Divide A by B, then add Response and 15.

Assignment is not the same as equality: assignment replaces the old value of the target variable with the results of the calculation.

Table 3-8.

C Jargon

Target = Response + 15 + A / B

- Target: The value to the left of the assignment operator is the l-val
- =: The assigment operator
- Response + 15 + A / B: The value to the right of the assignment operator is the r-val

L-vals can accept values being assigned to them. Usually, an l-val is the name of a variable. An r-val may involve computation, and hence one cannot assign a value to an r-val.

C compilers sometimes give error messages referring to l-vals and r-vals

Table 3-9.

Relational Operators

Relational operators let you compare the values of two variables using a specific comparison test. The result of such a test is either true or false.

In C, something is true if it has a non-zero value; something is false if it is zero.

==	Test for equality. NOTE: In C, assignment is a single equals sign, while the equality test is two equals signs together. Do not confuse them!
!=	Inequality
<	Less than
>	Greater than
<=	Less than or equal to
>=	Greater than or equal to

ble 3-20, as a way to escape to the statement immediately following the end of a loop.

Less often a program must begin a loop again from the beginning without finishing the loop body. C's *continue statement,* shown in Table 3-21, provides this mechanism.

Selection

Often a program must choose an action based on the value of an expression to evaluate. C's switch statement, Table 3-22, is a way to choose among many options based on the value of an expression. The switch statement avoids using many if-then statements.

ARRAYS, STRUCTURES, AND POINTERS

Arrays and *structures* are ways to store complex groups of data. They are

Table 3-10.

Logical Operators

Logical operators let you combine relational operators into complex tests. C gives you three logical operators:

A == B   &&   C < D

The logical AND operator

The result is true if both A equals B, and C is less than D.

A == B || C < D

The logical OR operator

The result is true if either A equals B, and C is less than D.

!   A == B

The logical NOT operator

The result is true if A equals B is false

very useful in common problems, as well as in sophisticated business and technical problems.

Arrays

Arrays, Table 3-23, are groups of variables which have the same data type. The elements in an array are numbered, and this *index number* allows the program to reference an element of the array.

Table 3-11.

Increment and Decrement Operators

Programs often add or subtract one from a variable. C provides special operators to do these tasks.

> Add one before the division.

Preincrement

```
B = B + 1 ;
A = B / 3 ;                A = ++B / 3 ;
```

becomes

```
A = B / 3 ;                A = B++ / 3 ;
B = B + 1 ;
```

> Add one after the division.

Postincrement

> Subtract one before the division

Predecrement

```
B = B - 1 ;
A = B / 3 ;                A = --B / 3 ;
```

becomes

```
A = B / 3 ;                A = B-- / 3 ;
B = B - 1 ;
```

> Subtract one after the division

Postdecrement

Table 3-12.

Combined Arithmetic and Assignment Operators

To simplify complex expressions, C provides a special set of operators that combine an arithmetic operator with assignment.

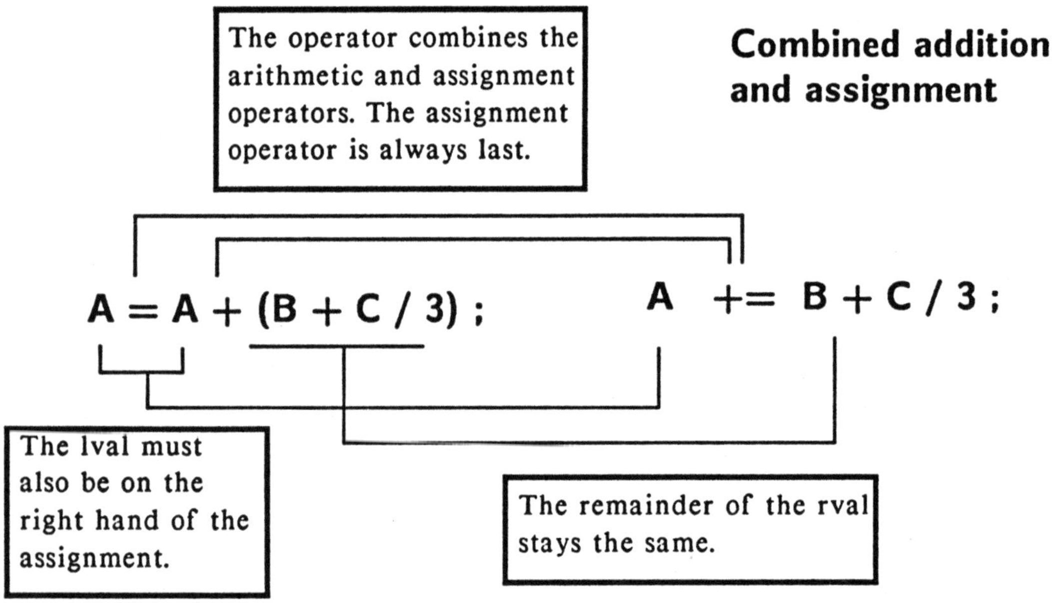

Operator	Meaning
+=	**Add and assign**
-=	**Subtract and assign**
*=	**Multiply and assign**
/=	**Divide and assign**
%=	**Modulus and assign**

Table 3-13.

Statements

A C statement is any C expression followed by a semicolon, or one of the control structures we will examine shortly.

The assignment statement is an example of a statement; here a semicolon follows an expression with the assignment operator. The assignment statement means to evaluate the right hand side of the assignment expression, and to place the result in the variable on the left hand side.

Table 3-14.

if Statements

C's if statement lets you execute a statement only if a particular expression is true.

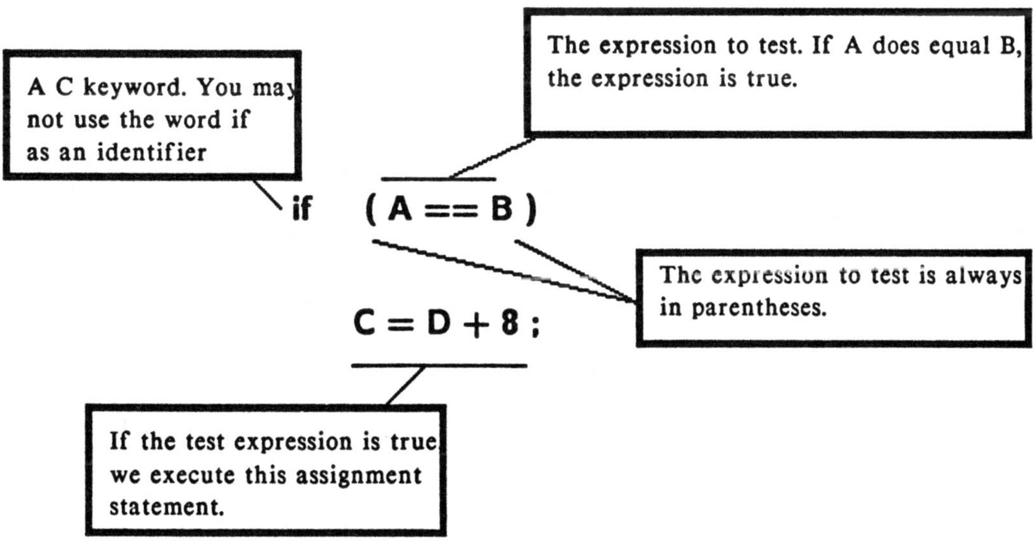

Table 3-15.

Compound Statements

Often the if statement needs to control more than a single statement. Enclosing a set of statements in curly brackets makes them behave as a single statement. Multiple statements bound together like this are called compound statements.

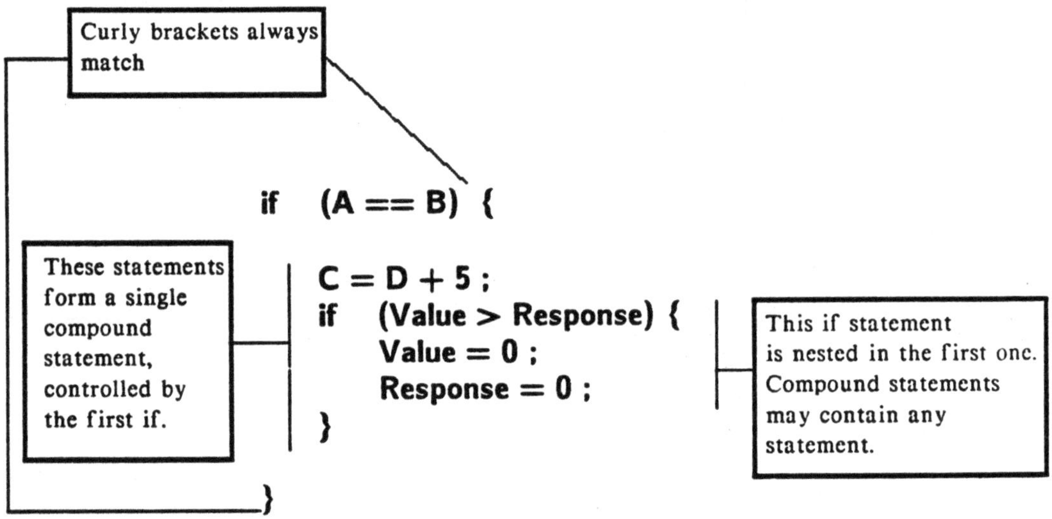

Character strings, Table 3-24, are arrays of characters. Strings have some special properties in C: not only can they store groups of individual characters, but they can store words, lines of text, or sentences. C also provides ways to work with a string as a single entity; see Table 3-25. The three library functions here are only a small part of the entire set of string functions.

Structures

While an array is a group of homogeneous data, a structure is a group of data, each element of which can have a different data type. See Table 3-26. Each element of a structure has a name, and this name, rather than a number index, accesses that part of the structure.

Table 3-27 shows how the *structure declaration* actually creates variables in memory. Table 3-28 then shows how C's *dot operator* accesses a field within a structure.

Table 3-16.

else Statements

The else statement executes if the condition specified in the if statement is false. else statements always pair with an if statement.

```
if   (A == B)  {
     Value = 0 ;
     Response = 0 ;
}
else   {
     Value = 15 ;
     Response = -5 ;
}
```

else statements always match with an if statement

If A does not equal B, the first compound statement does not execute. Instead, this second compound statement runs. else statements can have either a single or a compound statement.

Functions and Programs

A program written in C is a collection of C *functions and data declarations.* A *function* contains actual program code. Table 3-29 shows how a function appears. Functions take in data through parameters, and they can have privately declared data. The actual function statements appear inside the function. These statements only execute when the function is called by using its name in a program.

Table 3-30 shows how a C program is built from *data declarations,* the *main function,* and *auxiliary functions.* Every program must have a main function; the main function receives control from the operating system when the program begins to run. **main** can then call other functions defined in the program. It, or other functions, may also call functions defined in the standard C library of functions, provided as part of the compiler distribution.

Now, let's get down to the real pleasure of learning by doing: writing, compiling and running C programs.

Table 3-17.

while Loops

The while loop causes a statement to repeat as long as the specified condition remains true. The repeated statement can be a compound statement.

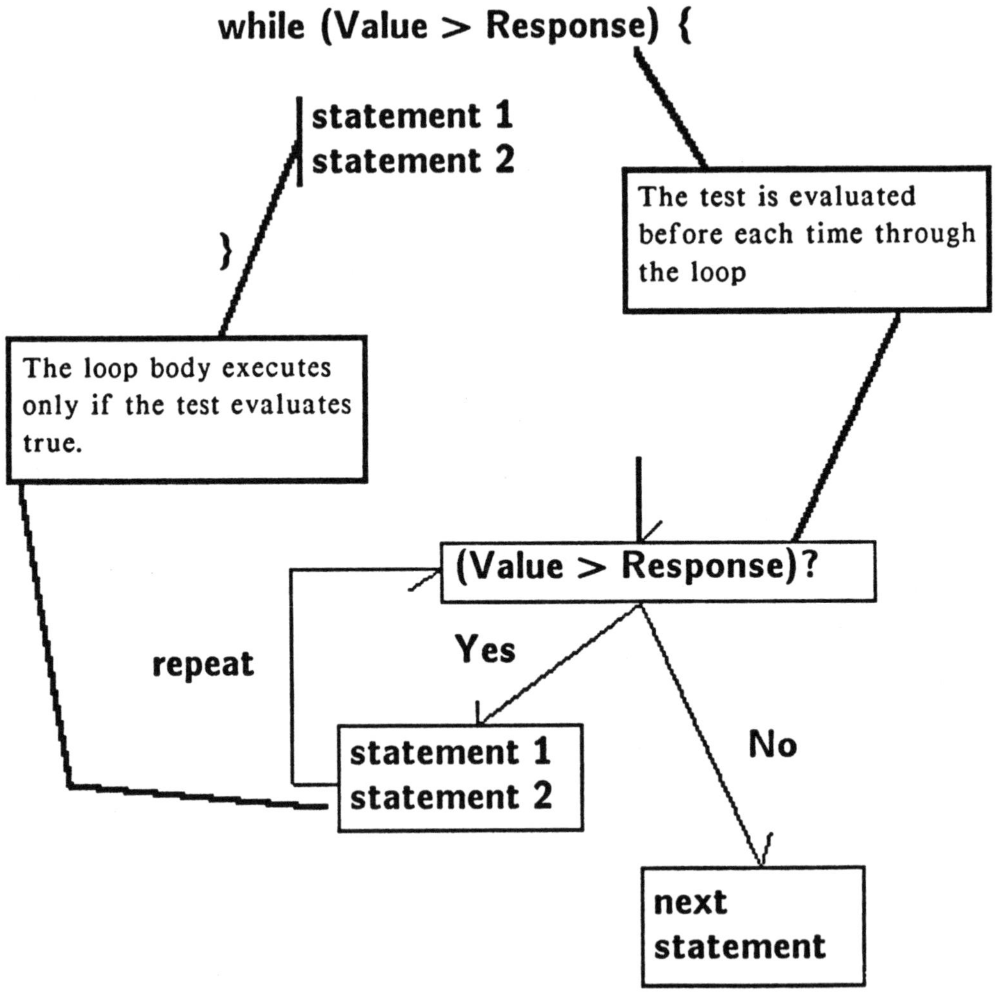

Table 3-18.

do-while Loops

The do- while loop causes a statement to repeat as long as the specified condition remains true. The repeated statement can be a compound statement. The do-while loop tests the condition at the end of the loop.

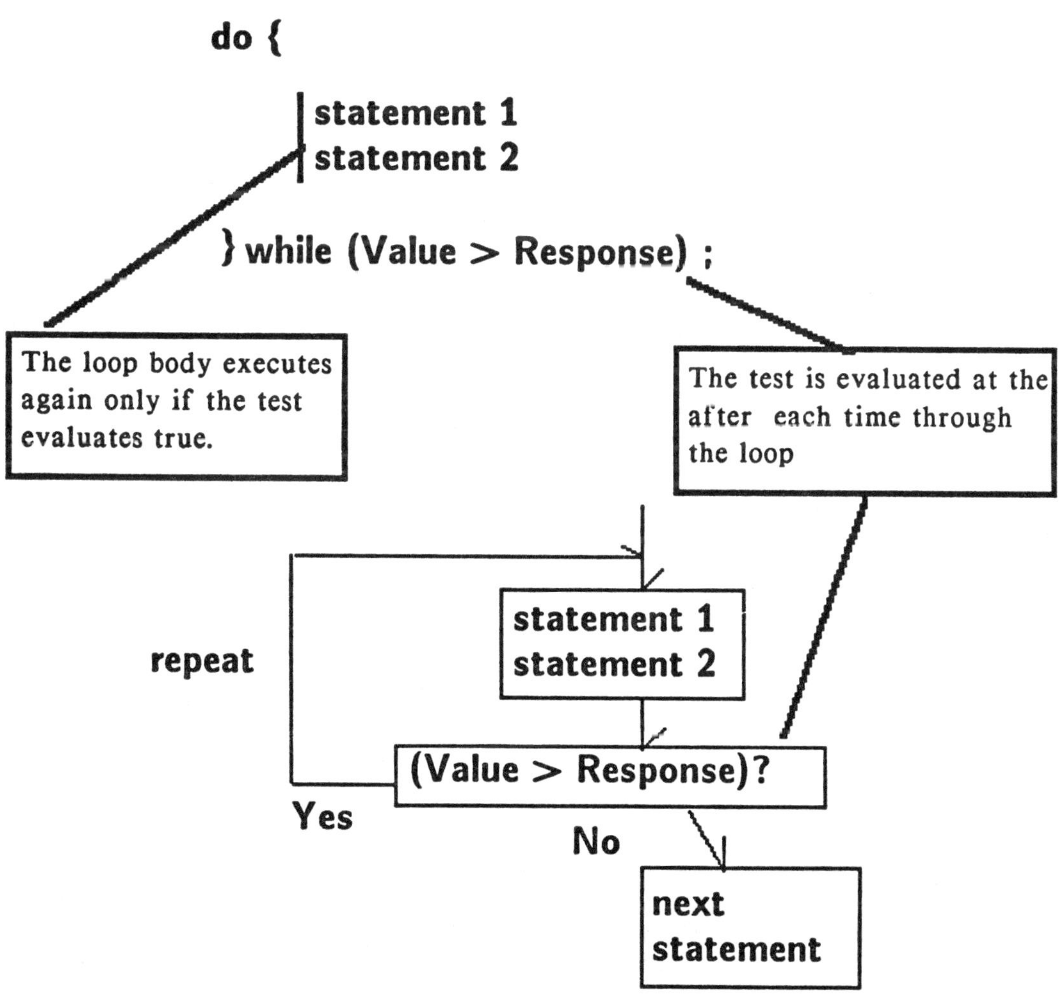

Table 3-19.

for Loops

The for loop is a shorthand notation for a while loop where the program first sets up the values of variables, and where variables are modified in a known way after each pass through the loop

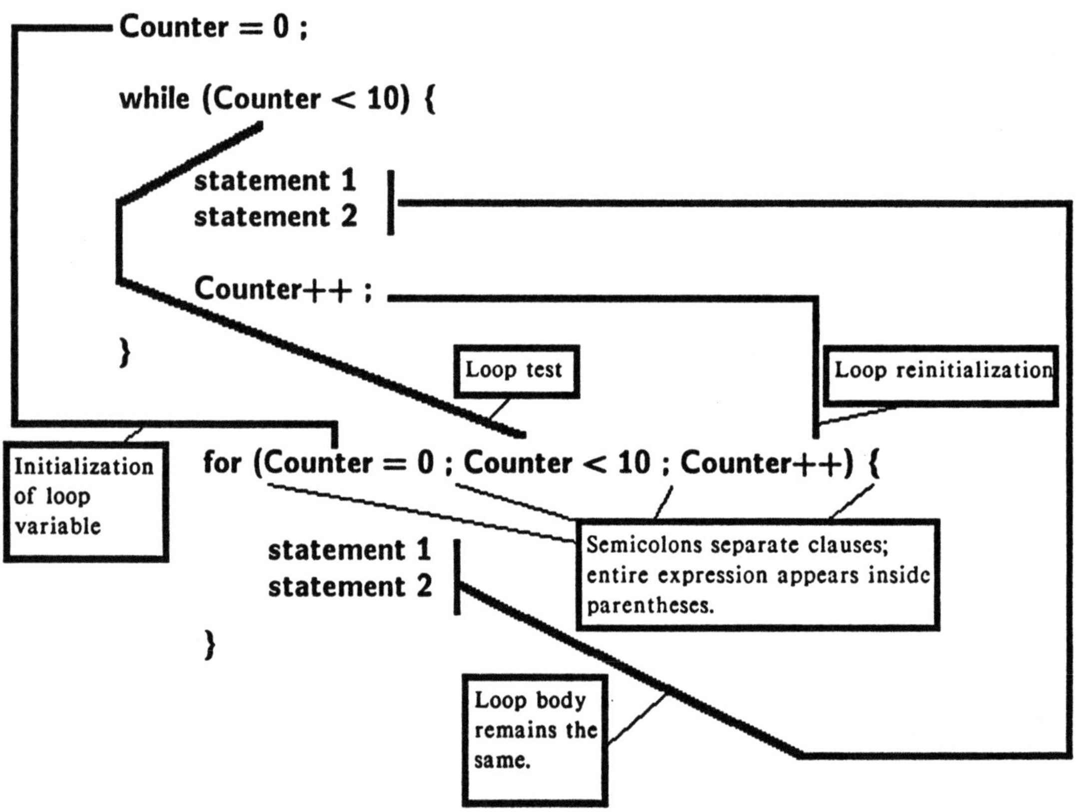

The loop reinitialization clause can be any C expression, but is usually an increment or decrement.

Table 3-20.

break

The break statement is a convenient way to leave a loop from any point inside.

```
while   (A == B) {

        Value = Average * 15 ;

        if (Value > QuarterlyPayment)
              break ;

        FinalPayment = Value / increment ;

}
```

Immediate exit to statement following

Table 3-21.

continue

The continue statement lets execution continue from the beginning of the loop again, short-circuiting the remainder of the loop.

```
while   (A == B) {

        Value = Average * 15 ;

        if (Value > QuarterlyPayment)
              continue ;

        FinalPayment = Value / increment ;

}
```

Execution continues from the top of the loop, beginning with the loop test.

Table 3-22.

switch Statement

To choose among a group of possible values, one could write a sequence of if statements. To simplify programs, C provides the switch statement.

```
switch (Value) {
    case 'a' :
        statements
        break ;

    case 'b':
    case 'c':
        statements
        break ;

    default:
        statements
}
```

Value: Expression to evaluate. The switch compares the value of this expression with each case selector

case 'a': If the selector is the letter 'a', the statements execute up to the break.

case 'b': / case 'c': If the selector is either the letter 'b' or the letter 'c', this set of statements execute up to the break

default: If no selector matches, the statements following the default selector execute. The default selector is optional.

Table 3-23.

Arrays in C

Arrays are groups of variables, each of which is the same type. Rather than have a unique name for each variable, an array has a single name, and identifying numbers for each array element. Such an identifying number is an array index.

Array Declaration

Square brackets indicate an array

```
int        IntegerArray [10] ;
```

Array base type. Each element in the array is an integer

The array name

The number of elements in the array

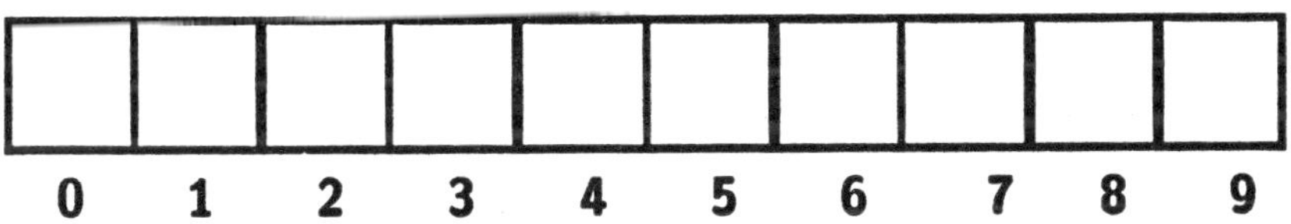

IntegerArray has ten elements, numbered zero through nine with their indices. Each element stores an integer.

To reference an array element, use the array name followed by the array index in square brackets.

```
IntegerArray[5] = IntegerArray[4] + 5 ;
IntegerArray[6]++ ;
```

Array elements can be lvals or part of an rval expression.

Table 3-24.

Character Strings

Character strings are arrays of characters that may be treated as a unit. Strings are useful for storing words, names, and any other group of characters that you want to treat together.

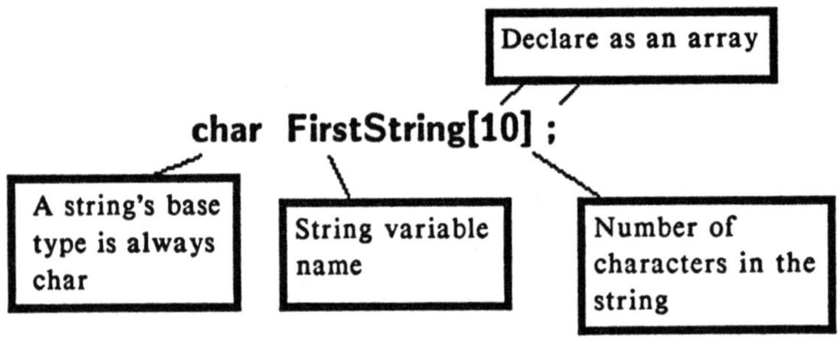

C always uses one of the array elements as an indicator of where the string ends. Programs can store strings of variable length, so long as the length is not more than one less than the declared length of the string.

The termination marker is a character whose value is all bits set zero (ASCII NUL). This is different from the zero character. In C programs, the terminator is written this way: '\0'. The digit zero is written this way: '0'.

FirstString

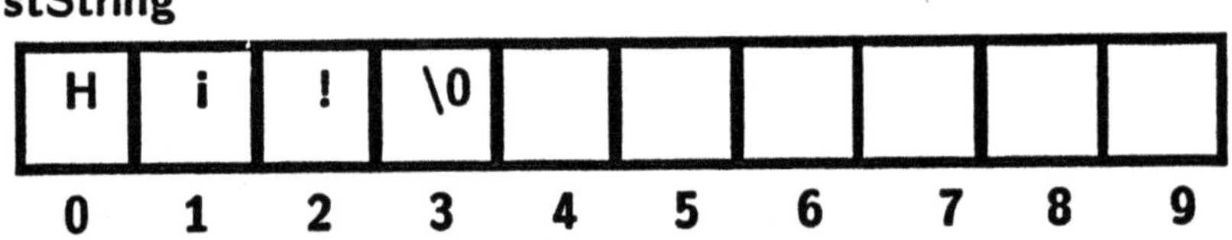

FirstString stores the value Hi!

Table 3-25.

Working with Strings

A string constant is any string enclosed in double quote marks.

"This is a string constant"

C automatically allocates memory to store the constant, and terminates the string with the zero marker.

Special string library functions:

strlen(String)	Returns the length of String as an integer
strcpy(Target,Source)	Copies the Source string into Target
strcat(Target,Source)	Adds the Source string to the end of the Target string

All these functions depend on having strings that obey the C standard: the end of every string must be marked with the terminating zero. strcpy and strcat add a terminator to the string they access. You must ensure that the Target string is declared large enough to store the result of strcpy and strcat.

Table 3-26.

Structures

While arrays are collections of items of the same data type, structures are collections of variables which need not have the same type. Array elements are referred to by their array index number, but structure elements are referred to by name.

Declaration

The name of this kind of structure

The struct keyword begins all structure declarations

```
struct EmployeeStructure {

    char Name[50] ;

    char SSN [9] ;

    long Salary ;

}
```

This structure has three fields, that hold the employee name, social security number, and salary. The name and SSN fields are character arrays, while the salary field is a long integer

Table 3-27.

More on Structures

With the previous structure template, we declare a structure in this way:

struct EmployeeStructure FirstEmployee ;

Previously defined structure name

Structure variable name

FirstEmployee is now a variable with three fields, Name, SSN, and Salary

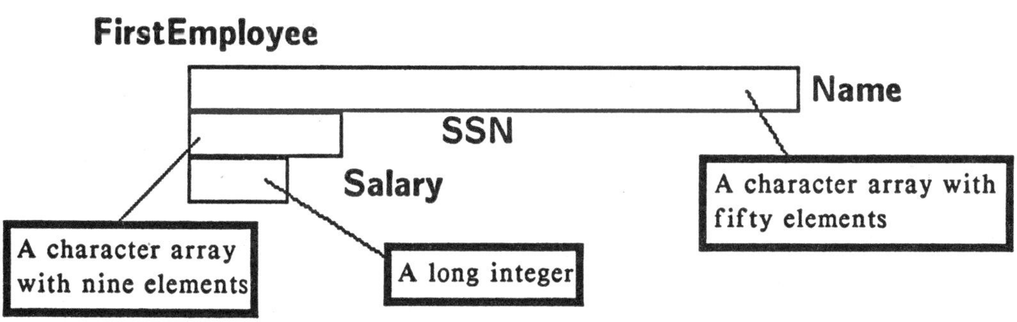

Table 3-28.

Using Structures

You access an array element with its element index number. You access a structure field element with its field name.

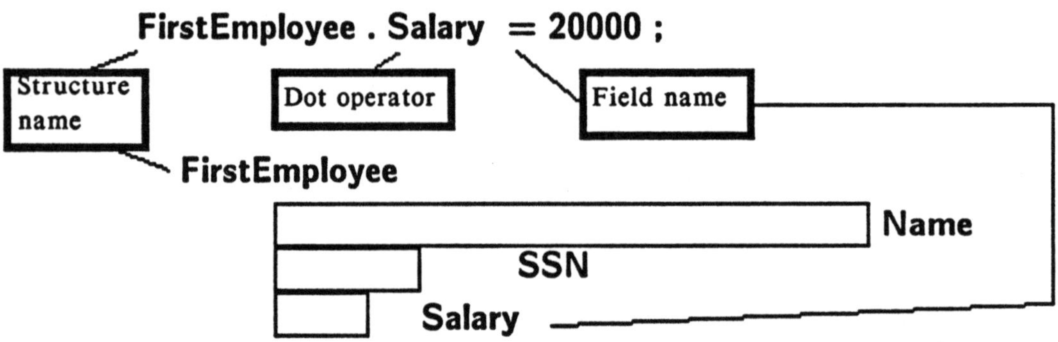

To access a field in a structure, use the structure name, the dot operator, and the structure field. This accesses the field as a variable. You may use such a structure expression as you would any variable.

Table 3-29.

C Functions

A C program is a collection of functions and data structures. The data structures are described in data declarations, while the functions are the actual C program code that executes.

The function name. You call a function by using the name in another function.

The list of function parameters. These are variables that provide input to the function.

The value the function returns is an int.

```
int strlen(String1)
char *String1 ;
{  /* strlen */
   function data declarations
   function statements
}  /* strlen */
```

Declarations of all parameters follow the function name

Here are declarations of variables known only inside this function

These statements are executed when the function is called

Table 3-3.

C Programs

A C program has many functions. One of these must be named main. The C run-time system calls main when it is ready to run the program. main, in turn, calls other functions in the program.

A typical program looks as follows:

```
Data declarations known
throughout the program

main()
{
   statements in main
}


function1( )
{
   statements in function1
}

. . .

              C program file
```

4

AGING: Accounts Receivable Analysis Program

All prudent business managers "age" their company's accounts receivable. The data that results from the process makes it possible for the financial manager to calculate the cost of money on the basis of "aging," which is the length of time it takes, on the average, to collect debts or accounts receivable.

Accounts receivable are the amounts owed to a business by its customers who have accepted deliveries of goods and services and for which the company has issued invoices and rightfully expects to be paid. On a balance sheet, accounts receivable are classed as current assets. However, these assets are not always convertible to cash because, in all business operations, some customers do not pay their bills. As a result, most companies deduct an allowance for bad debts from their total accounts receivable.

Bad debts are receivables that are never received, debts that are never paid despite all legal efforts to collect. A benefit of the account-aging process is the aid it provides in determining an allowance or the propriety of an allowance for bad debts.

Only sales made on credit are used to age accounts receivable. Cash sales cannot be aged. This does not usually present a problem—most businesses sell goods and services on credit terms. In these days of credit cards and extended payment terms, relatively few businesses operate on a strictly-cash basis.

On the basis of a finite period of time, with the total of sales known for this period, given the dollar value of all accounts receivable at the start and at the end of the time period, the AGING program instantly performs the calculations for the business manager who wants to know several important figures:

1. What is the accounts receivable turn-over ratio?
2. What is the average daily sales volume?
3. How many days does it take, on the average, to collect?

The receivables turn-over ratio indicates how many times, on average, receivables are generated and collected during the fiscal period. For example, if sales are $2,400,000 for the year, beginning receivables are $300,000, and year-end receivables are $500,000, receivable turn-over is computed by this formula:

$$\frac{\text{TOTAL SALES FOR THE YEAR}}{(\text{BEGINNING RECEIVABLES} + \text{YEAR END RECEIVABLES}) / 2} = \text{TURNOVER}$$

Using the numbers from our example:

$$\frac{2{,}400{,}000}{(300{,}000 + 500{,}000) / 2} = 6$$

The "turn-over" is a ratio that should be used for reference purposes: to compare the company's position with past history, or with the ratio achieved by a competitor, or with the ratio that may be considered average or typical for the industry.

The average daily sales volume is useful information for generating rolling-average calculations during a sales period to determine whether sales targets and goals are being met. If they are not being met, action can be taken before it is too late to develop strategies and to implement corrective tactics.

Let's do a sample run of the program AGING, Fig. 4-1. The boldface numbers represent our responses through the keyboard to the screen's requests for data.

Assume the program has been compiled and linked and the system prompt is displayed at the left edge of the screen. The system prompt is A> or B>, depending on which of the drives in a two-drive system is being accessed. The prompt means the system is ready for the next action from the keyboard. The compiled program is listed in the disk's directory as AGING.EXE. It is brought into action merely by typing all the characters in its name that are to the left of the decimal point. Thus, merely type the word AGING, press the Enter key and watch the screen for instructions.

The screen clears and program's name is displayed for a few seconds:

```
*******************************
AGING — Average Age of Receivables

*******************************
```

Fig. 4-1. Source code for AGING.

```
/* AGING - COPYRIGHT 1986 -  T. O. Sidebottom/L. A. Wortman       */

/*      Include Files (Don't forget the pound sign and you
        must start at column 1, the flush left margin)
*/
#include <stdio.h>

/*      External Declaration (Enter it exactly as shown)
*/
#include "utildefn.h"

/*      Main program
*/
main() {                          /* main */
    float   AREnd;                /* Accounts receivables at end of
                                  /* analysis period
                                  */
    float   ARStart;              /* Accounts receivables at start of
                                  /* analysis period
                                  */
    float   Period;               /* Number of days in analysis period
                                  */
    float   RecvTurnRat;          /* Calculated receivables-turnover
                                  /* ratio
                                  */
    float   Sales;                /* Net sales on credit for period
                                  */


    SignOn("AGING -- Average Age of Receivables", 20, 59, 9);

 /* Get starting information. (stdout is the console) */
    WriteSolidLine(stdout, 78, 0);
    printf("\n\t\t    COLLECTION PERIOD FOR ACCOUNTS RECEIVABLE\n\n");
    WriteSolidLine(stdout, 78, 0);
    printf("\n\t\t\t    (Credit Sales Only)\n\n");
    Prompt("How many DAYS are in the period you will compute?          ");
    scanf("%f", &Period);
    Prompt("\nWhat are the NET SALES ($) on credit for the period?      ");
    scanf("%f", &Sales);
    Prompt("\nEnter ACCOUNTS RECEIVABLE ($) at the START of the period: ");
    scanf("%f", &ARStart);
    Prompt("\nEnter ACCOUNTS RECEIVABLE ($) at the END of the period:   ");
    scanf("%f", &AREnd);
    printf("\n\n\n");

 /* Calculate the receivable turnover ratio. */
    RecvTurnRat = Sales / ((ARStart + AREnd) / 2);
 /* Print or List (Display) the report */
   printf("Average Accounts Receivable Turnover Ratio: %10.2f\n\n",
           RecvTurnRat);
```

```
    printf("Average Daily Sales for the Period:          %10.2f\n\n",
           Sales / Period);
    printf("Days Sales in Accounts Receivable:           %10.2f\n",
           Period / RecvTurnRat);
}                                   /* main */
```

Then the program's name is scrolled up and out of sight to be replaced by the following information displayed on the screen. Our responses to requests for data are entered at the keyboard and are shown here in boldface:

```
*******************************************
COLLECTION PERIOD FOR ACCOUNTS RECEIVABLE
*******************************************

              (Credit Sales Only)

How Many Days In the Period You Will Compute?           91
What Are the Net Sales ($) on Credit for the Period?    1000000
Enter Accounts Receivable at the Start of the Period:   300000
Enter Accounts Receivable at the End of the Period:     700000
```

When you press the Return or Enter key after making the last of the four entries, the information is calculated in a fraction of a second and is instantly displayed on the screen. Here is the management information generated and displayed on the screen as a result of the data entered in our example:

```
Average Accounts Receivable Turnover Ratio:                 2.00
Average Daily Sales for the Period:                     10989.01
Days Sales in Accounts Receivable:                         45.50
```

Our program in C asks the human operator for the data to be keyed in, accepts the data, processes it, and generates the display of the results of the computer's calculations.

Note that the very beginning of the source code includes **<stdio.h>** and **utildefn.h** *include* statements. **stdio.h** refers to a standard input/output file supplied as an important part of the compiler. Essentially, it steers or directs the source and the destination of information. The defaults are the computer keyboard as the source and the console's display or the video terminal as the destination. All programs in this book, and probably in all other books on using the C programming language with microcomputers (certainly for the popular IBM PC's), show the **include <stdio.h>** call or statement as the first instruction. **utildefn.h** is a programmer's shorthand or a file of text of commands common to a number of programs. Rather than rewrite the commands each time they are used, they are included in the source code. The actual content of the utildefn.h file, which you will create with your editor, is found in Appendix A.

5

AVGMED: Average and Median Calculations Program

This program demonstrates C functions, structures, and code for performing a number of diverse chores, including error-trapping, direction of output to screen and printer, float and integer handling, and calls to external functions.

The special importance of this program to the student and programmer in C is its ability to accept a reasonably large set of numbers, calculate their average and median values, sort the numbers in descending order, and provide both a screen display and a printed copy of the final data.

The code will accept a maximum input of 50 numbers. The actual quantity to be used for any specific run is determined by your response to the question the program asks:

```
How many numbers will you enter? (50 Max):
```

The maximum may be increased or decreased by revising the **#define** instruction under the heading "definitions," which initializes the variables, defines them or contains the initial values assigned to the variables. In this case, the name of the variable is MAXNUMVALUES:

```
#define MAXNUMVALUES 50
```

Change the number 50 to a larger or smaller value, as desired. The error trap will automatically adjust to the new value defined for MAXNUMVALUES. The definition for MINNUMVALUES is 2.

Here is a sample run of AVGMED, to demonstrate the interaction between the program's screen display and the user, with the user's responses shown in boldface:

How many numbers will you enter? (50 Max): **51**
You Entered a Number Greater than 50 or less than 2.
Please Re-Enter the Number: **12**

Enter Number 1:	**22.33**
Enter Number 2:	**44.56**
Enter Number 3:	**8.99**
Enter Number 4:	**35.67**
Enter Number 5:	**88.11**
Enter Number 6:	**67.43**
Enter Number 7:	**59.61**
Enter Number 8:	**74.77**
Enter Number 9:	**1.23**
Enter Number 10:	**.44**
Enter Number 11:	**98.98**
Enter Number 12:	**5.33**

Immediately after the 12th entry is made and the Enter or Return key is pressed, the program performs all the calculations and sends the following data to the screen:

Average = 42.29 Median = 29.00

Numbers in descending order:

98.99
88.11
74.77
67.43
59.61
44.56
35.67
22.33
8.99
5.33
1.23
0.44

At the same time, the output is sent to the printer, which reproduces the entire set of data, as shown in Fig. 5-2.

Fig. 5-1. Source code for AVGMED.

```
/* AVGMED -- COPYRIGHT 1985 by T. O. Sidebottom/L. A. Wortman

/* Include Files
*/
#include <stdio.h>

/*      Definitions ... initialize the variables
*/
#define FALSE   0
#define MINNUMVALUES  2
#define MAXNUMVALUES 50
#define MAXSTRLEN 255
#define PRINTERNAME "prn"
#define TRUE    1

/*      External Declarations
*/
#include "utildefn.h"

/*      Main program
*/
main() {                            /* main */
    float   Average = 0.0;          /* Mean value */
    int     Counter;                /* Loop index */
    int     HalfIndex;              /* Index of the median value */
    int     InnerCounter;           /* Loop index for sorting */
    int     LastMaxValueIndex;      /* Loop index for sorting */
    FILE * ListOut;                 /* Listing file, opened to printer */
    float   Median;                 /* Median value */
    int     NumValues;              /* Number of values to average */
    int     SortCounter;            /* Loop index for sorting */
    float   TransferVariable;       /* Temporary variable for sorting */
    float   Value[MAXNUMVALUES];/* Values to average */

 /* We first open the printer and display a startup banner. We then
    list a banner to the printer. If the program cannot access the
    printer, the "Can't open printer" error-message is displayed
    and the program is exited. */
    if (!(ListOut = fopen(PRINTERNAME, "w"))) {
        fprintf(stderr, "Can't open printer.");
        exit(0);
    }
   SignOn("AVERAGE/MEDIAN CALCULATOR", 23, 70, 0);
   ClearScreen();
   printf("\t\t *** TURN ON THE PRINTER ***\n\n\n");
   WaitFiveSeconds();
   ClearScreen();

   fprintf(ListOut, "       ════════════════════════════════════════\n");
   fprintf(ListOut, "                   AVERAGE/MEDIAN\n");
   fprintf(ListOut, "       ════════════════════════════════════════\n\n");
```

```
  /* We get the number of items we want to average, checking the number the
     user enters to ensure it is within an acceptable range. */
     printf("\n\n");
     Prompt("How many numbers will you enter? (50 Max): ");
     scanf("%d", &NumValues);
     printf("\n");
     fprintf(ListOut, "        Number of entries: %d\n\n", NumValues);
     while (NumValues > MAXNUMVALUES || NumValues < MINNUMVALUES) {
         printf("You Entered a Number Greater than %d or Less than %d.\n",
                 MAXNUMVALUES, MINNUMVALUES);
         Prompt("\nPlease Re-Enter the Number: ");
         scanf("%d", &NumValues);
         printf("\n");
     }

  /* Get the values. We prompt the user for each number and collect
     the value directly. The fflush call ensures that the prompt is
     displayed on the screen without needing a newline call. */
     for (Counter = 0; Counter < NumValues; Counter++) {
         printf("\tEnter Number %d: ", Counter + 1);
         fflush(stdout);
         scanf("%f", &Value[Counter]);
         fprintf(ListOut, "        Number %d = %8.2f\n",
                 Counter + 1, Value[Counter]);
     }
     printf("\n\n");

  /* Sort the numbers in descending order. We do a variant of a simple
     exchange sort. We always make NumValues - 1 pass through the
     values, exchanging disordered items as we go. */
     for (SortCounter = 0; SortCounter < (NumValues - 1);
             SortCounter++) {
         LastMaxValueIndex = SortCounter;
  /* We now scan through the values again, and compare each value with
     each other one. If we find a value out of order, we set the index
     of the value to exchange (LastMaxValueIndex) to that count. */
      for (InnerCounter = SortCounter + 1;
              InnerCounter < NumValues; InnerCounter++) {
          if (Value[LastMaxValueIndex] < Value[InnerCounter])
              LastMaxValueIndex = InnerCounter;
      }

  /* We now do the transfer by copying the value to the temporary
     variable (TransferVariable), and then exchanging the elements
     of the Value array. */
      TransferVariable = Value[SortCounter];
      Value[SortCounter] = Value[LastMaxValueIndex];
      Value[LastMaxValueIndex] = TransferVariable;
  }

/* Determine the median. */
   HalfIndex = NumValues / 2;
```

```
    /* If we have an even number of entries, average the two Value entries
       surrounding the middle.  Otherwise, take the middle Value. */
       Median = (NumValues % 2 == 0) ?
           (Value[HalfIndex] + Value[HalfIndex + 1]) / 2.0 :
           Value[HalfIndex];

    /* Determine the average. */
       for (Counter = 0; Counter < NumValues; Counter++)
           Average += Value[Counter];
       Average /= (float) NumValues;

    /* List results to the display. */
       printf("        ----------------------------------------\n");
       printf("        Average = %8.2f   Median = %8.2f\n", Average, Median);
       printf("        ----------------------------------------\n\n");
       printf("        Numbers in descending order:\n\n");
       for (Counter = 0; Counter < NumValues; Counter++)
           printf("                 %8.2f\n", Value[Counter]);
       printf("\n        ----------------------------------------\n");

    /* List results to the printer. */
       fprintf(ListOut,"\n        ----------------------------------------\n");
       fprintf(ListOut,"        Average = %8.2f   Median = %8.2f\n", Average, Median);

       fprintf(ListOut,"        ----------------------------------------\n\n");
       fprintf(ListOut,"        Numbers in descending order:\n\n");
       for (Counter = 0; Counter < NumValues; Counter++)
           fprintf(ListOut,"                 %8.2f\n", Value[Counter]);
       fprintf(ListOut,"\n        ----------------------------------------\n");
}                                   /* main */
```

Fig. 5-2. An actual printout of the results of running AVGMED.

```
========================================
            AVERAGE/MEDIAN
========================================

 Number of entries: 12

 Number 1 =    22.33
 Number 2 =    44.56
 Number 3 =     8.99
 Number 4 =    35.67
 Number 5 =    88.11
 Number 6 =    67.43
 Number 7 =    59.61
 Number 8 =    74.77
 Number 9 =     1.23
 Number 10 =     0.44
 Number 11 =    98.98
 Number 12 =     5.33
```

```
----------------------------------------
Average =     42.29   Median =     29.00
----------------------------------------

Numbers in descending order:

               98.98
               88.11
               74.77
               67.43
               59.61
               44.56
               35.67
               22.33
                8.99
                5.33
                1.23
                0.44
----------------------------------------
```

6

BARCHART: A Graphic Display of Data

Bar charts, also known as histograms, are among the most popular methods for displaying data. Representing or depicting data as bars laid side by side make it possible to instantly compare one unit of information with another.

Often a printer with graphics capabilities is needed to print the bars generated by histogram or bar chart programs. The BARCHART program works with any printer that can print the character X. The character X reproduced end-to-end in a quantity related to the size of the data to be depicted simulates a bar. If you prefer, a character other than the letter X may be used to represent the bar. Make this change by entering a character other than the X that appears in the definitions at the beginning of the source code in the line:

```
#define PLOTSYMBOL "X"
```

Wherever the variable PLOTSYMBOL appears in the source code it is replaced by the value (the character) assigned to it:

```
printf(PLOTSYMBOL) ;
fprintf (Printer,PLOTSYMBOL) ;
```

The **printf** line determines what will be sent to or displayed on the screen. The **fprintf** line determines the character that will be recognized by the printer. The asterisk symbol, or the uppercase letter O, are often used in histogram displays. Choose one that satisfies you.

Fig. 6-1. Source code for BARCHART.

```
/* BARCHART - Copyright 1986 - T. O. Sidebottom/L. A. Wortman      */

/*      Include Files
*/
#include <stdio.h>

/*      Definitions
*/
#define HEIGHT  30
#define PLOTSYMBOL "X"   /* Here is where the plot-character
                            is identified.  Change it if you
                            prefer something other than "X" */
#define PRINTERNAME     "prn"

/*      External Declarations
*/
#include "utildefn.h"

/*      Main program
*/
main(argc, argv) {                  /* main */
    FILE * Printer;                 /* File opened to the printer */
    int     SymbolCounter;          /* The symbol for the BARs is defined by
                                       the name PLOTSYMBOL. You may choose any
                                       other printable symbol you want. */
    float   Value;                  /* Value to be plotted */

 /* Open the printer and clear the screen in preparation for input.
    If the printer cannot be addressed by the program, an error
    message is displayed and the program is exited.  */
    if (!(Printer = fopen(PRINTERNAME, "w"))) {
        fprintf(stderr, "Check the printer, please.");
        exit(0);
    }
    ClearScreen();
 /* Continue accepting input and plotting it until the user enters a
    minus-one. The while condition at the loop's end controls exit from
    the loop. */
    do {

    /* Prompt the user for input, and read the incoming data. */
        printf("\nEnter the LENGTH of the BAR.\n");
        Prompt("(Enter -1 to END the Program):   ");
        scanf("%f", &Value);

    /* If the value is within range, plot it. */
        if ((Value >= 0) && (Value < 101.0)) {

        /* Print the value as a number at the beginning of each line. */
            printf("%6.2f : ", Value);
            fprintf(Printer, "%6.2f : ", Value);
```

```
        /* Print and display the PLOTSYMBOL the correct number of
           times by cycling through the following loop Value/2 times.
           We divide the integer of Value by 2 to keep it within
           the borders for width, which is usually 80 maximum. */
            for (SymbolCounter = 0; SymbolCounter < (int) Value / 2;
                    SymbolCounter++) {
                printf(PLOTSYMBOL);
                fprintf(Printer, PLOTSYMBOL);
            }

        /* Start a new line. */
            printf("\n");
            fprintf(Printer, "\n");
        }

    /* If the value is out of range, and not minus-one (end of data),
       signal an error. */
        else
            if (Value != -1)
                printf("\n>>> Length must be 100 or less <<<\n");
    } while (Value > 0);
}                                   /* main */
```

After the code has been processed and the executable BARCHART.EXE program has been created by the compiler/linker, type the command **BARCHART** and press the Enter or Return key. The screen clears and the following instruction appears at the bottom of the screen; (our responses through the keyboard are in boldface):

Enter the LENGTH of the BAR.
(Enter −1 to END the Program) : **33**

As soon as you type the length of the bar and press return, the screen displays the digits for "LENGTH of the BAR" you keyed in, and a related linear display of the character:

33.00 : XXXXXXXXXXXXXXXX

The request for a new entry is again displayed:

Enter the LENGTH of the BAR.
(Enter −1 to END the Program): **44.50**

The immediate response is:

22.50 : XXXXXXXXXXX

The program continues:

```
Enter the LENGTH of the BAR.
(Enter -1 to END the Program) :     22.50
44.50  :  XXXXXXXXXXXXXXXXXXXXXX
```

The invitation to enter the length of the bar is displayed again at the screen. When finished with the entries, type **-1** and press Return. Instantly, the printer produces the following bar chart, which combines all the entries we've made:

```
33.00  :  XXXXXXXXXXXXXXXX
22.50  :  XXXXXXXXXXX
44.50  :  XXXXXXXXXXXXXXXXXXXXXX
```

The program rejects lengths of bars that are above 100. If you enter a number greater than 100, an error message will be displayed:

```
>>>Length must be 100 or less <<<
```

The size of this greater-than length may be changed at the following line in the source code:

```
if( (Value >=0) && (Value <101.0) ) {
```

To deal with maximum-size quantities greater or smaller than 100.0 change the value **101.0** to whatever length you prefer. Also, for cosmetic purposes, change the error message to coincide with the new maximum length. To keep the length of the bar from wrapping around the printed page or the screen, select another digit to replace the divisor (2) in the following line of source code:

```
for (SymbolCounter = 0 ; SymbolCounter < (int)Value / 2;
    SymbolCounter++) {
```

Figure 6-2 is a typical printout of a bar chart generated by the program, after the source code has been compiled to produce the file BARCHART.EXE.

Fig. 6-2. An actual printout generated by BARCHART.

```
 33.00 : XXXXXXXXXXXXXXXX
 22.50 : XXXXXXXXXXX
 44.50 : XXXXXXXXXXXXXXXXXXXXXX
 12.12 : XXXXXX
 23.35 : XXXXXXXXXXX
 29.83 : XXXXXXXXXXXXXX
 36.00 : XXXXXXXXXXXXXXXXXX
 43.25 : XXXXXXXXXXXXXXXXXXXXX
 87.00 : XXXXXXXXXXXXXXXXXXXXXXXXXXXXXXXXXXXXXXXXXXX
 95.50 : XXXXXXXXXXXXXXXXXXXXXXXXXXXXXXXXXXXXXXXXXXXXXXX
100.00 : XXXXXXXXXXXXXXXXXXXXXXXXXXXXXXXXXXXXXXXXXXXXXXXXXX
 90.00 : XXXXXXXXXXXXXXXXXXXXXXXXXXXXXXXXXXXXXXXXXXXXX
 80.00 : XXXXXXXXXXXXXXXXXXXXXXXXXXXXXXXXXXXXXXXX
 70.00 : XXXXXXXXXXXXXXXXXXXXXXXXXXXXXXXXXXX
 60.00 : XXXXXXXXXXXXXXXXXXXXXXXXXXXXXX
 50.00 : XXXXXXXXXXXXXXXXXXXXXXXXX
 40.00 : XXXXXXXXXXXXXXXXXXXX
 30.00 : XXXXXXXXXXXXXXX
 20.00 : XXXXXXXXXX
 10.00 : XXXXX
  5.00 : XX
  2.00 : X
  0.00 :
```

7

BKEVN: Break-Even Analysis Program

Break even is the point in a financial statement for a product or service where total sales revenues equal total costs. At the break-even point there is neither profit nor loss. When preparing a sales forecast or planning a production level for a product, it is important to know how many units have to be sold to reach the break-even point and a profit will commence to be generated. This is also true for companies or individuals who sell services. BKEVN, Fig. 7-1, is a rapid and highly accurate program that deals with financial variables and dynamics and determines the break-even point.

We will start with three data items: the total fixed costs (costs that are incurred without regard to the number of units sold or produced); the variable costs per unit (costs that are directly related to each unit produced and, hopefully, sold); and the selling price per unit. From these three items BKEVN will calculate, display and print the exact point in which the sales dollars are equal to the total costs. The program also displays a table which gives the value of the loss below, and the amount of gain above, the break-even point. This kind of information is fundamental, and essential to the development of a forecast for marketing, manufacturing, and financial planning.

Here is a typical run of the program (with responses to the screen's questions shown in boldface), and the table of data that is generated, displayed at the screen and, if desired, printed:

```
Enter the TOTAL FIXED COSTS?             100000
Enter the VARIABLE COSTS per UNIT?       1234.56
Enter the SELLING PRICE per UNIT?        2345.67
```

Fig. 7-1. Source code for BKEVN.

```
/* BKEVN - COPYRIGHT 1986 - T. O. Sidebottom/L. A. Wortman  */

/*      Include Files
*/
#include <stdio.h>              /* stdio.h comes with the compiler */
#include <ctype.h>              /* so does the ctype.h file */

/*      Typedefs
*/
typedef struct dType {
    float   FixedCost;          /* Fixed costs in producing item */
    float   VariableCost;       /* Variable costs in producing item */
    float   SellPrice;          /* Item selling price */
    int     StartQuan;          /* Starting production quantity */
    int     EndQuan;            /* Ending production quantity */
    int     IncrQuan;           /* Number to increment in quantity
                                   analysis */
}

/* The type DataType contains all the data values we store.
   DataPtr is the type pointing to DataTypes. */
     DataType, *DataPtr;

/*      External Declarations
*/
#include "utildefn.h"          /* include it so we don't
                                  have to retype it */


/*      Function Feclarations
*/
void GenerateReport();
DataPtr GetData();

/*      Main Program
*/
main(argc, argv)
int     argc;
char   *argv[];
{                               /* main */
    FILE * ListOut;             /* File opened to printer */
    int     Response;           /* Receives character input from user */
    DataPtr Value;              /* Contains our analysis input */
                                                                      }
/* We print the signon banner, get initial data, and then clear
   the screen in preparation for the analysis. */
   SignOn("BKEVN - Calculate Breakeven Points", 25, 53, 15);

   Value = GetData();
   WaitASecond();
   ClearScreen();

/* Here we print our results to the display until the user
```

```
   enters a character other than a 'y' or 'Y'. */
   do {
       GenerateReport(stdout, Value);
       printf("\nRepeat the display? (Y/N): ");
       fflush(stdout);
       scanf("%1s", &Response);

   /* If the Response character is in upper case, the tolower
      function converts the character to lower case. */
   } while (tolower(Response) == 'y');

/* We now optionally list the results to the printer. */
   printf("\n\nPrintout?  Turn on the printer.");
   Prompt(" Then, type 'Y' or 'N':    ");
   scanf("%1s", &Response);

/* The user wants a printed listing. We first open the printer. */

   if (tolower(Response) == 'y') {
       if (!(ListOut = fopen("prn", "w"))) {
           fprintf("Check the printer, please. I can't open it!");
           exit(0);
       }
   /* And then print the report again and again until the user
      enters a 'Y' or 'y'. Note that we can use the same report
      generation routine for both the screen and the printer
      because we pass the file to use for printing as a
      parameter to GenerateReport. */
       do {
           GenerateReport(ListOut, Value);
           Prompt("Repeat the printout?  'Y' or 'N': ");
           scanf("%1s", &Response);
       } while (tolower(Response) == 'y');
   }
}                                  /* main */

/* Prepare the report from the input data Value and list the
   results to the file OutFile. */
void GenerateReport(OutFile, Value)
DataPtr Value;
FILE * OutFile;
{                                  /* GenerateReport */
    float    BreakEven;            /* The breakeven point */
    float    CostBrkEven;          /* Total costs at the breakeven
                                      point */
    int      CurQuantity;          /* Counter representing the current
                                      unit quantity */
    float    FixedCost;            /* Fixed startup costs */
    float    ProfLoss;
    float    RevBrkEven;           /* Revenue at break even */
    float    TotalCost;            /* Total production costs */
    float    TotalSales;           /* Total sales */
    float    UnitCost;             /* Final cost per unit */
    int      BkevnQty;             /* Breakeven quantity */


 /* First write the startup banner */
```

```
   WriteSolidLine(OutFile, 62, 2);
   fprintf(OutFile,
          "\n");
   fprintf(OutFile,"                              BREAKEVEN DISPLAY\n\n");
   WriteSolidLine(OutFile, 62, 2);
   fprintf(OutFile,"\n");
   fprintf(OutFile," QTY     TOTAL COST    TOTAL SALES      ");
   fprintf(OutFile,"GAIN/LOSS     UNIT COST\n\n");
   WriteSolidLine(OutFile, 62, 2);
   fprintf(OutFile,           "\n");

/* Calculate intermediate values. */
   BreakEven = Value -> FixedCost /
       (Value -> SellPrice - Value -> VariableCost);
   RevBrkEven = Value -> SellPrice * BreakEven;
   CostBrkEven = Value -> FixedCost +
       (Value -> VariableCost * BreakEven);

/* Now list the results. */
   for (CurQuantity = Value -> StartQuan;
          CurQuantity <= Value -> EndQuan;
          CurQuantity += Value -> IncrQuan) {
       TotalSales = Value -> SellPrice * (float) CurQuantity;
       TotalCost = Value -> FixedCost +
           (Value -> VariableCost * (float) CurQuantity);
       UnitCost = TotalCost / (float) CurQuantity;
       ProfLoss = TotalSales - TotalCost;
       BkevnQty = Value -> FixedCost /
           (Value -> SellPrice - Value -> VariableCost);
       fprintf(OutFile,
               " %3d   %12.2f   %12.2f   %12.2f  %12.2f\n",
               CurQuantity, TotalCost, TotalSales,
               ProfLoss, UnitCost);
   }
   WriteSolidLine(OutFile, 62, 2);
   fprintf(OutFile," %3d   %12.2f   %12.2f = BREAKEVEN POINT\n",
          BkevnQty, CostBrkEven, RevBrkEven);
   WriteSolidLine(OutFile, 62, 2);
   fprintf(OutFile, "\n");
   fprintf(OutFile,"  TOTAL FIXED COST:          %12.2f\n",
          Value -> FixedCost);
   fprintf(OutFile,"  VARIABLE COSTS PER UNIT:  %12.2f\n",
          Value -> VariableCost);
   fprintf(OutFile,"  SELLING PRICE PER UNIT:   %12.2f\n\n",
          Value -> SellPrice);
   WriteSolidLine(OutFile, 62, 2);
   fflush(OutFile);
}                              /* GenerateReport */

/* The GetData function returns a pointer to a filled-in
   data structure with the input data. */
     DataPtr GetData() {              /* GetData */
     DataPtr NewData;

 /* We create a DataType element by calling malloc, the memory
```

```
    allocation function. It returns a pointer to a region of
    memory for our data. We return this pointer at the end of
    this function. We test to ensure we've got a good allocation;
    malloc returns NULL if the allocation fails. */
    if ((NewData = (DataPtr) malloc(sizeof(DataType))) == NULL) {
        fprintf(stderr, "Out of memory in GetData.");
        exit(1);
    }

/* Still inside the GetData function, we "get" or display
    requests for the input data from the keyboard. */
    Prompt("          Enter the TOTAL FIXED COSTS:   ");
    scanf("%f", &NewData->FixedCost);
    Prompt("\nEnter the VARIABLE COSTS per UNIT:   ");
    scanf("%f", &NewData->VariableCost);
    Prompt("\n Enter the SELLING PRICE per UNIT:   ");
    scanf("%f", &NewData->SellPrice);
    printf("\n\n\n");
    printf("GIVE THE FOLLOWING FOR COMPUTATION ...\n");
    Prompt("\n      Enter the Starting Quantity:   ");
    scanf("%d", &NewData->StartQuan);
    Prompt("\n        Enter the Ending Quantity:   ");
    scanf("%d", &NewData->EndQuan);
    Prompt("\n     And the Incremental Quantity:   ");
    scanf("%d", &NewData->IncrQuan);
    printf("\n\n\n");
    return(NewData);
}                               /* GetData */
```

ENTER THE FOLLOWING FOR COMPUTATION. . .

Starting Quantity:	10
Ending Quantity:	150
Incremental Quantity:	10

Choose the starting, ending, and incremental quantity levels for the computer to calculate and display. It may be necessary to try several different combinations to find the combination of quantities that provide the desired table of data, which includes information above and below the break-even point. The program also creates a table of data that helps you figure out exactly how much you may be losing or gaining at various levels of production—a sort of "what-if" game that can be played as an aid to forecasting sales, production, and financial conditions.

After the table of data is displayed, you are invited to make a printed copy merely by responding to the question "Printout?" and entering a **Y** or an **N**. (Of course the printer must be turned on.) Figure 7-2 is the actual table of data, based on the above entries.

Fig. 7-2. An actual printout produced by BKEVN.

```
**************************************************************

                     BREAKEVEN DISPLAY

**************************************************************

QTY     TOTAL COST    TOTAL SALES       GAIN/LOSS      UNIT COST

**************************************************************


 10      112345.60       23456.70       -88888.91       11234.56
 20      124691.20       46913.40       -77777.80        6234.56
 30      137036.80       70370.09       -66666.70        4567.89
 40      149382.41       93826.80       -55555.61        3734.56
 50      161728.00      117283.50       -44444.50        3234.56
 60      174073.61      140740.19       -33333.42        2901.23
 70      186419.20      164196.89       -22222.31        2663.13
 80      198764.81      187653.59       -11111.22        2484.56
 90      211110.41      211110.30           -0.11        2345.67
100      223456.00      234567.00        11111.00        2234.56
110      235801.61      258023.69        22222.08        2143.65
120      248147.20      281480.38        33333.17        2067.89
130      260492.81      304937.09        44444.28        2003.79
140      272838.41      328393.78        55555.38        1948.85
150      285184.00      351850.50        66666.50        1901.23
**************************************************************
 90      211110.53      211110.53 = BREAKEVEN POINT
**************************************************************

TOTAL FIXED COST:              100000.00
VARIABLE COSTS PER UNIT:         1234.56
SELLING PRICE PER UNIT:          2345.67

**************************************************************
```

8

CHKACCT: Checking Account Analysis Program

Here is a menu-driven program (a selection of actions is offered from which you make choices), Fig. 8-1, that enables you to keep an accurate and up-to-date record of the activities in your checking account. A printed copy of the deposits and withdrawals is created by the program. If your account reaches an overdrawn point, a warning message is displayed on the screen.

Whether or not you consider a checking-account program easier to use than a manual check register is not important. The important thing is to see how various computer-controlled functions can be accomplished through the proper use of the C code.

The program starts with a request for the date. In this run-through, each of our responses to questions the program displays on the screen are shown in boldface:

```
What is the DATE of the First Transaction?
            (Use the Format MM/DD/YY):                    7/01/86

What is the DATE of the Last Transaction?
            (Use the Format MM/DD/YY):                    7/31/86

What is the Beginning ($) Balance?                       12345.67
```

Now the menu from which you choose the type of transaction is displayed:

Fig. 8-1. Source code for CHKACCT.

```
/* CHKACCT - COPYRIGHT 1986 - T. O. Sidebottom/L. A. Wortman    */

/*      Include Files
*/
#include <stdio.h>
#include <ctype.h>

/*      Definitions
*/
#define FALSE   0
#define MAXSTRLEN 255
#define PRINTERNAME "prn"
#define TRUE    1

/*      External Declarations
*/
#include "utildefn.h"

/*      Function Declarations
*/
float   MakeDeposit();
void StartingConditions();
void WrapUp();
float   WriteChecks();

/*      Global Variables
*/
float   Balance;              /* Current checking balance */
float   CheckAmt;             /* Check amount */
char    EndPeriod[MAXSTRLEN]; /* String containing user's description
                                 of analysis period */
FILE * ListOut;               /* File opened to printer */
char    SelectChar[2];        /* Receives input characters from the user */


/*      Main Program
*/
main() {                              /* main */

 /* We first open the printer. If the open fails, we print an error
    message and terminate immediately. */
    if (!(ListOut = fopen(PRINTERNAME, "w"))) {
        fprintf(stderr, "Check the printer, please.");
        exit(1);
    }

 /* We next print the login banner and collect the account
    conditions at the start of the analysis. */
    SignOn("CHKACCT - BUSINESS CHECKING ACCOUNT", 15, 72, 0);
    StartingConditions();
```

```
/* We next receive transactions from the user. The user may want a
   checking deposit, a withdrawal, or to stop the analysis. We call
specific functions to collect data for each of these cases. */
do {
    printf("\nTo enter the total of the deposit..Type 'D'\n");
    printf("To enter total of checks written...Type 'C'\n");
    printf("To Quit............................Type 'Q'\n");
    Prompt("\nSelect D, C, or Q: ");
    scanf("%1s", SelectChar);

/* Based on the value entered, we choose one of the following
   "cases" as represented by the letters d, c, and q. */
    switch (SelectChar[0] = tolower(SelectChar[0])) {
        case 'd':
        /* We collect information about the account balance in
           MakeDeposit */
            Balance = Balance + MakeDeposit();
            break;

        case 'c':
        /* We collect information about checks in WriteChecks */
            Balance = Balance - WriteChecks();
            break;

        case 'q':
            break;

        default:
            printf("\nERROR...Please re-enter the selection!\n");
    }
   /* We display and print the ending balance, and indicate
      if the account is overdrawn. */
       if (SelectChar[0] == 'd' || SelectChar[0] == 'c') {
           printf("\nAfter this transaction, the balance Is: $%9.2f\n\n",
                   Balance);


           fprintf(ListOut,"\nAfter this transaction, the balance Is: $%9.2f\n\n",
                   Balance);
           if (Balance < 0.0) {
               printf("\n===> THE ACCOUNT IS OVERDRAWN! <===\n\n");
               fprintf(ListOut,"\n===> THE ACCOUNT IS OVERDRAWN! <===\n\n");
           }
       }

    } while (SelectChar[0] != 'q');
    WrapUp();
}                                 /* main */

/* MakeDeposit gets deposit information. It records the transaction
   in the listing and returns the deposit information to the caller. */
float   MakeDeposit() {           /* MakeDeposit */
    float   DepAmt;
    char    DepDate[MAXSTRLEN];
    char    JournalRef[MAXSTRLEN];
```

```
 /* We clear the screen and collect the date, the amount of deposit,
    and references to the deposit. Note the date and references are
    stored in character strings. */
    ClearScreen();
    Prompt("What is the DATE of the deposit? ");
    fgets(DepDate, MAXSTRLEN, stdin);
    fgets(DepDate, MAXSTRLEN, stdin);
    Prompt("\nWhat is the ($) AMOUNT of the deposit? ");
    scanf("%f", &DepAmt);
    printf("\nWhat are the JOURNAL or LEDGER references? \n");
    Prompt("(Put a space between entries): ");
    fgets(JournalRef, MAXSTRLEN, stdin);
    fgets(JournalRef, MAXSTRLEN, stdin);

 /* We list the deposit information. */
    fprintf(ListOut, "\nRECORD OF DEPOSITS\n");
    fprintf(ListOut, "------------------\n\n");
    fprintf(ListOut, " The %s deposit is: $%9.2f", DepDate, DepAmt);
    fprintf(ListOut, "\n Journal or ledger references are: %s\n", JournalRef);
 /* And return the deposit amount. */
    return(DepAmt);
}                               /* MakeDeposit */

/* Get the first and last transaction dates and the beginning balance. */
void StartingConditions() {     /* StartingConditions */
    char    StartPeriod[MAXSTRLEN];
    char    StopPeriod[MAXSTRLEN];

 /* We get a description of the analysis period, and
    the starting balance. */
    printf("What is the DATE of the first transaction?\n");
    Prompt("         (Use the format MM/DD/YY): ");
    fgets(StartPeriod, MAXSTRLEN, stdin);
    StripReturns(StartPeriod);
    printf("\nWhat is the DATE of the last transaction?\n");
    Prompt("         (Use the format MM/DD/YY): ");
    fgets(StopPeriod, MAXSTRLEN, stdin);
    StripReturns(StartPeriod);
    Prompt("\nWhat is the beginning ($) balance? ");
    scanf("%f", &Balance);

 /* We then list a banner on the printer. */
    fprintf(ListOut, "==============================================\n")
    fprintf(ListOut, "\nTHE PERIOD OF THIS REPORT IS FROM %s",
            StartPeriod);
    fprintf(ListOut, " TO %s\n", StopPeriod);
    fprintf(ListOut, "\n===> THE BEGINNING BALANCE IS: $%10.2f <===\n", Balance);
}                               /* StartingConditions */

/* WrapUp writes the ending balance information to both the display
   and to the printer */
void WrapUp() {                 /* WrapUp */
    printf(" \n===> THE ENDING BALANCE IS: $%9.2f <===\n", Balance);
    fprintf(ListOut, "\n===> THE ENDING BALANCE IS: $%9.2f <===\n\n", Balance);
```

```
    fprintf(ListOut, "=-=-=-=-=-=-=-=-=-=-=-=-=-=-=-=-=-=-=-=-=-=-=-=-=-=-=-=-=-=-=-=\n")
}                                  /* WrapUp */
/* Write the checks and return the debited amount. */
float   WriteChecks() {          /* WriteChecks */
    char    CheckNumbers[MAXSTRLEN];
    char    NumChecks[MAXSTRLEN];
/* We clear the screen, and get the total dollar amount
   of checks written. */
   ClearScreen();
   Prompt("What is the ($) amount of checks written? ");
   scanf("%f", &CheckAmt);

/* Now we collect information on the actual checks. Note that
   the check numbers are stored in character string variables.
   The first fgets call clears the input buffer to read
   following lines properly. */
   fgets(NumChecks, MAXSTRLEN, stdin);
   Prompt("\nHow many checks were written? ");
   fgets(NumChecks, MAXSTRLEN, stdin);
   printf("\nWhat are the checks' numbers?\n");
   Prompt("(Put a space between entries): ");
   fgets(CheckNumbers, MAXSTRLEN, stdin);

/* The routine ends by sending this information to the printer,
   and returning the check amount to the caller. */
   fprintf(ListOut, "\nRECORD OF CHECKS WRITTEN\n");
   fprintf(ListOut, "----------------------\n\n");
   fprintf(ListOut, " Total amount of checks written: $%9.2f\n", CheckAmt);
   fprintf(ListOut, " Number of checks written: %s\n", NumChecks);
   fprintf(ListOut, " The numbers of the checks are: %s\n", CheckNumbers);
   return(CheckAmt);
}                                  /* WriteChecks */
```

```
To Enter the Total of the Deposit .......................Type 'D'
To Enter Total of Checks written.........................Type 'C'
To QUIT..................................................Type 'Q'

Select D, C, or Q:     D
```

Because you selected the D option, the program asks pertinent questions about the deposit:

```
What is the DATE of the deposit?                        7/10/86
What is the ($) AMOUNT of the deposit?                  8123.47
What are the JOURNAL or LEDGER references?
(Press the SPACE BAR between entries):
12A.34  13B.44  14C.56  23C.66
```

The program responds with an update on the screen, adding the 5/10/85 deposit of $8123.47 to the opening balance of $12345.67, and shows:

After this Transaction, the Balance Is: $20469.14

The menu reappears. This time select "C." The questions at the screen now are concerned with the checks that have been written against the account:

What is the ($) Amount of Checks Written? **21543.33**
How Many Checks Were Written? **6**
What Are the Checks' Numbers?
(Press the SPACE BAR between entries): **101 102 103 104 105 106**

The screen displays the new total. Because the balance is negative a warning message is also displayed:

After this Transaction, the Balance Is: $ −1074.19
===> THE ACCOUNT IS OVERDRAWN!<===

Fig. 8-2. An actual printout generated by CHKACCT.

```
THE PERIOD OF THIS REPORT IS FROM 7/01/86 TO 7/31/86

===> THE BEGINNING BALANCE IS: $  12345.67 <===

RECORD OF DEPOSITS
------------------

 The 7/10/86
 deposit is: $  8123.47
 Journal or ledger references are: 12A.34 13B.44 14C.56 23C.66

 After this transaction, the balance Is: $ 20469.14


RECORD OF CHECKS WRITTEN
------------------------

 Total amount of checks written: $ 21543.33
 Number of checks written: 6

 The numbers of the checks are: 101 102 103 104 105 106

 After this transaction, the balance Is: $ -1074.19


===> THE ACCOUNT IS OVERDRAWN! <===

===> THE ENDING BALANCE IS: $ -1074.19 <===
```

This advises you that on the date of the last transaction the account was overdrawn. The menu reappears at the screen, from which you can make new entries. If additional deposits have been made to cover the amount of the overdraft, the CHKACCT program will accept this information and, when you press "Q" to quit or exit the program, the ending balance will be calculated and displayed as a positive amount. If the overdraft has not been adjusted, the overdraft will be displayed appropriately as a negative ending balance.

Figure 8-2 is a series of checking account activities shown in a printout produced by the program.

9

CNTALL: Counting Words, Sentences and Lines of Text

Professional writers often must prepare their manuscripts to fit specific space requirements. People who have to write an article for the company's newsletter are asked for a certain number of words to fit an allocated space. Experienced writers of speeches can translate numbers of written words into time required for the speaker to deliver the speech. Programmers want to know how many lines of code they have written for a program. Some people are curious about how many key strokes they have entered for work done with a word processor. Others are interested in how many sentences they have written. The reasons this kind of information is needed are varied and personal. CNTALL, the C program that is the subject of this chapter (see Fig. 9-1) is designed to provide a rapid response.

This program differs from others in this book in that it does not have a sign-on banner and does not ask a single question. All interaction is at the *command line* (the line entered at the system prompt). For example, suppose we want to get a quick line count of the source code for CNTALL itself. Here is the information we enter at the command line:

```
cntall cntall.c
```

Approximately six seconds after you press the enter key, this is the set of data displayed at the screen:

Fig. 9-1. Source code for CNTALL.

```
/* CNTALL - COPYRIGHT 1986 by T. O. Sidebottom/L. A. Wortman  */

/*      Include Files
*/
#include <stdio.h>
#include <ctype.h>

/*      Definitions
*/
#define BOOL int
#define CARRIAGE_RETURN 0x0D      /* Note the underscore character */
#define FALSE   0
#define MAXSTRLEN 255
#define LINE_FEED 0x0A            /* Again, the underscore */
#define PRINTERNAME "prn"
#define TRUE    1

/*      External declarations
*/
#include "utildefn.h"

/*      Main program
*/
main(argc, argv)
int     argc;
char   *argv[];
{                                 /* main */
    int     CurChar;              /* Current character being processed */
    FILE * InFile;                /* Input file */
    BOOL InWord = FALSE;          /* Flag set true if we're inside a word */
    int     NumChars = 0;         /* Number of characters in file */
    int     NumLines = 0;         /* Number of lines in file */
    int     NumSent = 0;          /* Number of sentences in file */
    int     NumWords = 0;         /* Number of words in file */
    char    Temp;                 /* Temporary variable */

 /* CNTALL needs an input filename specified on the command line.
    If the user forgets to enter the filename, the command line is
    incomplete or incorrect; the count of the number of arguments
    is less than 2.  If this is the situation, we display a message
    describing the correct program usage, and we gracefully exit
    the program, returning to the DOS prompt. */
   if (argc < 2) {
       printf("Didn't you forget to enter a file name?\n");
       printf("Use: cntall filename <CR>\n");
       exit(1);
   }
```

```
/* Open the file and, if it cannot be found, display a message and
   exit to the DOS prompt.  */
   if (!(InFile = fopen(argv[1], "r"))) {
       printf("I can't find %s. It may not be on this disk!\n", argv[1]);
       exit(0);
   }

/* Read the file a character at a time.  This program includes
   special processing for WordStar text files.  If the program
   sees a CARRIAGE_RETURN, it looks for a LINE_FEED as the
   following character.  If so, this is a normal MS-DOS end of
   line sequence; we throw away the LINE_FEEED.  If not, it may
   be a special sequence introduced by a word processor, such as
   WordStar. */
   while ((CurChar = getc(InFile)) != EOF) {
       if (CurChar == CARRIAGE_RETURN) {
           if ((Temp = getc(InFile)) == LINE_FEED)
           /* This is a real end-of-line.
              Throw away CARRIAGE_RETURN. */
               CurChar = Temp;
           else      /* Not a sequence; put back the character. */
               ungetc(Temp, InFile);
       }

   /* A non-whitespace means a visible character.  Count it. */
       if (!isspace(CurChar))
           NumChars++;

   /* Count sentences by counting sentence-ending
      punctuation marks. */
       if (CurChar == '.' || CurChar == '!' || CurChar == '?')
           NumSent++;

   /* Count lines by counting newlines. */
       if (CurChar == '\n')
           NumLines++;
   /* Count words by looking for movement from a non-word
      to a word.  A word begins with a non-whitespace
      character, and ends with the next whitespace character.
      We set the variable InWord to FALSE.  If InWord is
      false, and we find a character inside a word, we count
      the word and set InWord to TRUE.  InWord lets us count
      the first character, but no subsequent ones.  When we
      leave the word, InWord is again set to FALSE.  */
       if (isspace(CurChar))
           InWord = FALSE;
       else
           if (!InWord) {
               InWord = TRUE;
               NumWords++;
           }
   }
```

```
/* Report the statistics. */
   printf("\n\n\t\tDATA FOR FILE: %s\n", argv[1]);
   printf("\t\t--------------------------------\n");
   printf("\t\tChar Count: %d\n", NumChars);
   printf("\t\tLine Count: %d\n", NumLines);
   printf("\t\tWord Count: %d\n", NumWords);
   printf("\t\tSent Count: %d\n", NumSent);
}                                  /* main */
```

```
DATA FOR FILE:     cntall.c
------------------------------------------------
Char Count:  2004
Line Count:  94
Word Count:  390
Sent Count:  29
```

In this example, the Word Count is actually a count of the spaces between groups of characters in the source code. (For every word there must be a space.) The last data item, Sent Count, counts the number of sentences by counting periods, question marks, and exclamation points in the (cntall.c) file.

Error-trapping is incorporated in the program. For example, if you call for the CNTALL program at the command line but forget or neglect to enter the name of the file to be counted (uppercase or lowercase letters may be used), the following error message is displayed:

```
A>cntall
Didn't you forget to enter a file name?
Use: cntall filename <CR>
```

If you enter an incorrect file name, a message is displayed to remind you to recheck your entry:

```
A>cntall zzz
I can't find zzz. It may not be on this disk!
```

Let's count the words in this chapter (not including the source code), which was given the filename "chap9.ms." (The word processor's nonprinting commands will also be counted.)

Enter the following at the command line (in any combination of uppercase or lowercase characters):

```
cntall chap9.ms
```

Press enter and the program produces the display of statistics. (Note that the name of the file whose data is being analyzed will appear in uppercase or lowercase, depending on which you used when entering the file name at the command line.):

```
DATA FOR FILE:     chap9.ms
-------------------------------------------------------------------
Char Count:  2744
Line Count:  117
Word Count:  589
Sent Count:  22
```

10

CONVERT: Rapid Metric-Standard-Metric Conversion Program

While controversy and confusion may continue for some time, the ability to make conversions from metric to English (also known as *standard*) measurements and the converse is important to many of us. It's not too difficult to make the conversions—if you know thc formulas. Howcvcr, it can bc painstaking to make the conversions when you need or are seeking some degree of precision. The computer's ability to make precise as well as rapid calculations is ideally suited to a program such as Fig. 10-1, CONVERT.

The program is completely menu-driven. That is to say, a menu or list of 25 selections (including "End the Program") is displayed on the screen. You choose the appropriate number from the menu and press Enter. If you should inadvertently choose a number less than one or greater than 25 the screen will display a notice that you have made an error:

```
>>> OUT OF RANGE <<<
```

After a few seconds delay, the message automatically scrolls up and off the screen. It is replaced by the menu, Fig. 10-2, which occupies the entire screen, from which you make selections of the conversions to be calculated.

When you select a number in the range of 1 – 24, the screen displays a request for a quantity. For example, select item number 18 from the menu and the following is the interaction, with our responses to requests for data shown in boldface:

Fig. 10-1. Source code for CONVERT.

```
/* CONVERT -- COPYRIGHT 1986 by T. O. SIDEBOTTOM/L. A. WORTMAN  */

/*      Include Files
*/
#include <stdio.h>

/*      Definitions
*/
#define TRUE    1

/*      External declarations
*/
#include "utildefn.h"

/* Forward declarations
*/
void ConvertQuantity();
void DisplayMenu();

/*      Main program
*/
main(argc, argv) {                  /* main */
    int     Choice;

 /* First print a signon banner */
    SignOn("CONVERT METRICS to STANDARD to METRICS", 20, 50, 15);

 /* Continue displaying the menu and collecting a desired conversion
    number from the user until 25 (stop run) is entered. */
    while (TRUE) {
        DisplayMenu();
        WriteSolidLine(stdout, 69, 4);

    /* Collect the choice */
        Prompt("\n                        Select 1 to 25: ");
        scanf("%d", &Choice);

    /* Ending the run */
        if (Choice == 25)
            break;
        if (Choice < 1 || Choice > 25) {
        /* Value is out of range. Signal an error and begin from
           the top of the loop */
            printf("\n\n                       >>> OUT OF RANGE <<<\n");
            WaitASecond();
            continue;
        }

    /* Otherwise, perform the conversion. */
        ConvertQuantity(Choice);
    }
 }                                  /* main */
```

```
/* Perform the desired conversion. */
void ConvertQuantity(Choice)
int     Choice;
{                                   /* ConvertQuantity */
    float   Quantity;               /* Value to be converted */
    char    TestChar;               /* Temporary variable */

 /* Collect the input value */
    Prompt("\n                      Enter the Quantity to Be Converted: ");
    scanf("%f", &Quantity);
    printf("\n                      ");

 /* Perform the conversion, using the input parameter Choice to
    select the conversion formula; use the "case" structure. */
    switch (Choice) {
        case 1:
            printf("%7.2f Inches = %7.2f Millimeters\n",
                    Quantity, Quantity * 25.4);
            break;

        case 2:
            printf("%7.2f Inches = %7.2f Meters\n",
                    Quantity, Quantity * 0.0254);
            break;

        case 3:
            printf("%7.2f Feet = %7.2f Meters\n",
                    Quantity, Quantity * 0.3048);
            break;

        case 4:
            printf("%7.2f Miles = %7.2f Kilometers\n",
                    Quantity, Quantity * 1.6093);
            break;

        case 5:
            printf("%7.2f Teaspoons = %7.2f Milliliters\n",
                    Quantity, Quantity * 5.0);
            break;

        case 6:
            printf("%7.2f Tablespoons = %7.2f Milliliters\n",
                    Quantity, Quantity * 15);
            break;

        case 7:
            printf("%7.2f Pints = %7.2f Liters\n",
                    Quantity, Quantity * 0.4732);
            break;

        case 8:
            printf("%7.2f Quarts = %7.2f Liters\n",
                    Quantity, Quantity * 0.9463);
            break;
```

```
case 9:
    printf("%7.2f Gallons = %7.2f Liters\n",
            Quantity, Quantity * 3.7853);
    break;

case 10:
    printf("%7.2f Ounces = %7.2f Grams\n",
            Quantity, Quantity * 28.3495);
    break;

case 11:
    printf("%7.2f Pounds = %7.2f Kilograms\n",
            Quantity, Quantity * 0.453);
    break;

case 12:
    printf("%7.2f Degrees Fahrenheit = %7.2f Degrees Celsius\n",
            Quantity, (Quantity - 32.0) * 5.0 / 9.0);
    break;

case 13:
    printf("%7.2f Millimeters = %7.2f Inches\n",
            Quantity, Quantity * 0.0394);
    break;

case 14:
    printf("%7.2f Meters = %7.2f Inches\n",
            Quantity, Quantity * 39.37);
    break;

case 15:
    printf("%7.2f Meters = %7.2f Feet\n",
            Quantity, Quantity * 3.2808);
    break;

case 16:
    printf("%7.2f Kilometers = %7.2f Miles\n",
            Quantity, Quantity * 0.6214);
    break;

case 17:
    printf("%7.2f Milliliters = %7.2f Teaspoons\n",
            Quantity, Quantity * 0.2);
    break;

case 18:
    printf("%7.2f Milliliters = %7.2f Tablespoons\n",
            Quantity, Quantity * 0.0667);
    break;

case 19:
    printf("%7.2f Liters = %7.2f Pints\n",
            Quantity, Quantity * 2.1134);
    break;
```

```
        case 20:
            printf("%7.2f Liters = %7.2f Quarts\n",
                    Quantity, Quantity * 1.0567);
            break;

        case 21:
            printf("%7.2f Liters = %7.2f Gallons\n",
                    Quantity, Quantity * 0.2642);
            break;

        case 22:
            printf("%7.2f Grams = %7.2f Ounces\n",
                    Quantity, Quantity * 0.0353);
            break;

        case 23:
            printf("%7.2f Kilograms = %7.2f Pounds\n",
                    Quantity, Quantity * 2.2046);
            break;

        case 24:
            printf("%7.2f Degrees Celsius = %7.2f Degrees Fahrenheit\n",
                    Quantity, (Quantity * 9.0 / 5.0) + 32.0);
            break;

        case 25:
            break;
    }
    printf("\n        >>> Press any letter and the Enter key to continue <<< \n");
    scanf("%1s", &TestChar);
}                               /* ConvertQuantity */

/* DisplayMenu writes the available conversion choices to the display. */
void DisplayMenu() {            /* DisplayMenu */
    ClearScreen();
    WriteSolidLine(stdout, 69, 4);
    printf("                        METRICS/STANDARD/METRICS MENU\n");
    WriteSolidLine(stdout, 69, 4);
    printf("\n");
    printf("     1 - Inches to Millimeters          ");
    printf("13 - Millimeters to Inches\n");
    printf("     2 - Inches to Meters               ");
    printf("14 - Meters to Inches\n");
    printf("     3 - Feet to Meters                 ");
    printf("15 - Meters to Feet\n");
    printf("     4 - Miles to Kilometers            ");
    printf("16 - Kilometers to Miles\n");
    printf("     5 - Teaspoons to Milliliters       ");
    printf("17 - Milliliters to Teaspoons\n");
    printf("     6 - Tablespoons to Milliliters     ");
    printf("18 - Milliliters to Tablespoons\n");
    printf("     7 - Pints to Liters                ");
    printf("19 - Liters to Pints\n");
    printf("     8 - Quarts to Liters               ");
    printf("20 - Liters to Quarts\n");
```

```
    printf("      9 - Gallons to Liters                 ");
    printf("21 - Liters to Gallons\n");
    printf("     10 - Ounces to Grams                   ");
    printf("22 - Grams to Ounces\n");
    printf("     11 - Pounds to Kilograms               ");
    printf("23 - Kilograms to Pounds\n");
    printf("     12 - Fahrenheit to Celsius             ");
    printf("24 - Celsius to Fahrenheit\n");
    printf(
      "                                          25 - End the Program\n\n");
}                              /* DisplayMenu */
```

```
**********************************************************************
                    METRICS/STANDARD/METRICS MENU
**********************************************************************

  1 - Inches to Millimeters           13 - Millimeters to Inches
  2 - Inches to Meters                14 - Meters to Inches
  3 - Feet to Meters                  15 - Meters to Feet
  4 - Miles to Kilometers             16 - Kilometers to Miles
  5 - Teaspoons to Milliliters        17 - Milliliters to Teaspoons
  6 - Tablespoons to Milliliters      18 - Milliliters to Tablespoons
  7 - Pints to Liters                 19 - Liters to Pints
  8 - Quarts to Liters                20 - Liters to Quarts
  9 - Gallons to Liters               21 - Liters to Gallons
 10 - Ounces to Grams                 22 - Grams to Ounces
 11 - Pounds to Kilograms             23 - Kilograms to Pounds
 12 - Fahrenheit to Celsius           24 - Celsius to Fahrenheit
                                      25 - End the Program

**********************************************************************
```

Fig. 10-2. The display of the menu generated by CONVERT.

```
        Enter the Quantity to Be Converted:   23.45
             23.45 Milliliters = 1.56 Tablespoons
   >>> Press Any Letter and the Enter key to Continue <<<
```

The CONVERT program does not make a printed copy; however, if you are using the IBM PC, XT or AT, or a compatible with the print-screen capability, you can press the Shift-PrtSc keys to obtain a printed copy of all screen displays, including the menu, your selections for conversions, the units or quantity you enter and that are to be converted, and the converted quantity.

Select number 25, press Enter, and the system prompt appears instantly, signaling that the program has been terminated.

11

DAYWEEK: Conversion from Numeric Date to Day of the Week

A short, yet very interesting program, DAYWEEK (Fig. 11-1) demonstrates the speed and power of C to accept numeric information as input and convert it to text strings. A printed copy is not provided by the code. However, the simplicity and clarity of the code offers an opportunity for exercise in adding code that will also direct output to the printer (*prn, 1st,* for examples) as well as to the console (*con*), depending on the syntax recognized by your compiler and your hardware's configuration.

When you compile the source code and run the program, the screen is cleared, *scrolled* actually, by a series of 30 *newlines* (carriage returns and line feeds). This is the purpose of the function **ClearScreen,** which is called from UTILS.C. A sign on banner is displayed for approximately one second:

```
**********************
   Day-Of-The-Week
**********************
```

The screen is cleared again, and the following appears on the screen:

```
Enter a date . . . the day of the week
will be calculated and displayed.
Enter the month as two digits (MM) :    13
```

Oops! We goofed and made an impossible entry for the number of the month.

Fig. 11-1. Source code for DAYWEEK.

```
/* DAYWEEK -- COPYRIGHT 1986 by T. O. Sidebottom/L. A. Wortman   */

/* Include Files
*/
#include <stdio.h>

/*      Definitions
*/
#define FALSE   0
#define MINFACTOR  1
#define MAXFACTOR 12
#define MAXSTRLEN 255
#define TRUE    1

/* External declarations
*/
#include "utildefn.h"

/*      Global variables
*/
char   *DayNames[] = {           /* A list of the days of the week */
    " ",
    "Sunday",
    "Monday",
    "Tuesday",
    "Wednesday",
    "Thursday",
    "Friday",
    "Saturday"
};

int     Factor[] = {
    0, 1, 4, 4, 0, 2, 5, 0, 3, 6, 1, 4, 6
};

/* Main program
*/
main() {                         /* main */
    int     Day;                 /* Input day */
    int     Month;               /* Input month */
    int     Year;                /* Input year */
    int     Temp;                /* Temporary variable */

/* Write a login banner, and then print the user's instructions. */
   ClearScreen();
   SignOn("Day-Of-The-Week", 25, 63, 0);

   ClearScreen();
   printf("Enter a date . . . the day of the week\n");
   printf("will be calculated and displayed.\n\n\n");
   Prompt("Enter the month as two digits (MM): ");
   scanf("%d", &Month);
```

```
/* This error trap stops entering a non-existent month */
   while ((Month > MAXFACTOR) || (Month < MINFACTOR)) {
       printf("\nSorry! There is no such month! Please re-enter!\n");
       Prompt("\nEnter the month as two digits (MM): ");
       scanf("%d", &Month);
   }

   Prompt("Enter the day as two digits (DD):   ");
   scanf("%d", &Day);
   Prompt("Enter the year as two digits (YY):  ");
   scanf("%d", &Year);

   Temp = (Year / 4) + Year;

   Temp += Factor[Month];
   Temp += Day;
   Temp %= 7;

   printf("\n\n\t   The day of the week is: %s\n\n", DayNames[Temp]);
}                                /* main */
```

An error trap catches this and displays the message:

Sorry! There Is No Such Month! Please Re-Enter!

Enter the month as two digits (MM): **12**
Enter the day as two digits (DD): **31**
Enter the year as two digits (YY): **85**

When the enter key is pressed after the YY entry has been made, the screen instantly displays the message:

The day of the week is: Wednesday

The above series asked for the day of the week represented by New Year's Eve, December 31, 1986. The program can be used to determine the day of the week for any date in the past or the future in the 20th century.

12

DEPREC3: Depreciation Tables Program

The correct calculation of depreciation charges for fixed or capital assets are important to the determination of a business operation's Federal tax situation. An asset-acquisition is assigned a life expectancy under classifications defined by the Internal Revenue Service. The asset must be depreciated over a period of time not less than the period given in the guidelines of the IRS. It cannot be "expensed" all at once.

There are numerous methods for calculating the amount that may be depreciated during specific time or fiscal periods. It is neither practical nor realistic for us to publish all the methods and provide computer programs that deal with the complexities of depreciation, or with the dynamics of the IRS decision-making regulation-changing processes. Therefore, we have limited Fig. 12-1, DEPREC3, to the three diverse and most frequently used methods: straight line (SL); sum-of-years-digits (SOYD); and declining balance (DB).

After the sign-on banner is displayed and the screen is cleared, requests are made for information. Our responses in this sample run are shown in boldface. First, a request for information:

Type the Name of the Asset to Be Depreciated: **ABC**

The program continues:

On One Line, Describe the Asset—ABC:
Dot-Matrix Printer with Serial Interface

Fig. 12-1. Source code for DEPREC3.

```
/* DEPREC3 - COPYRIGHT 1986 by T. O. Sidebottom/L. A. Wortman  */

/*      Include Files
*/
#include <stdio.h>

/*      Definitions
*/
#define BOOL int
#define DECLINEBAL 1
#define FALSE   0
#define MAXSTRLEN 255
#define PRINTERNAME "prn"
#define STRAIGHTLINE 0
#define SUMYEARSDIGITS 2
#define TRUE    1

/*      External declarations
*/
#include "utildefn.h"

/* Forward declarations
*/
void StartingConditions() ;
void WriteHeading() ;
void WritePrinterBanner() ;
void WriteValue() ;

/*      Global variables
*/
float   AcquisCost;               /* Item's acquisition cost */
float   BookValue;                /* Item's book value */
float   CumDeprec;                /* Cumulative depreciation amount */
float   CurrentYr;                /* Current year */
float   DBFactor;                 /* Declining balance factor */
char    ItemDescr[MAXSTRLEN];     /* Item description */
char    ItemName[MAXSTRLEN];      /* Item's name */
FILE * ListOut;                   /* File opened to printer */
float   ScrapValue;               /* Final scrap value */
float   StraightLn;               /* Straight line value */
int     UsefulLife;               /* Years of useful life */
float   YrsLeft;                  /* Number of years left */
/*      Main program
*/
main(argc, argv)
int     argc;
char   *argv[];
{                                 /* main */
    int     Count;

 /* Open the printer. If the open fails, print a message
    and stop */
```

```
    if (!(ListOut = fopen(PRINTERNAME, "w"))) {
        fprintf(stderr, "Can't open printer.");
        exit(1);
    }

/* Print a login message, and ge the starting conditions.
    Print a banner on the printer. */
    SignOn("DEPREC3 -- THREE-METHOD DEPRECIATION TABLES", 20, 50, 15);
    StartingConditions();
    WritePrinterBanner();

/* Perform the straight-line analysis. Write a heading.
    Describe the depreciation, and print the analysis. */
    WriteHeading(stdout, STRAIGHTLINE);
    WriteHeading(ListOut, STRAIGHTLINE);
    CumDeprec = 0.0;
    WriteValue(stdout, 0, 0.0, 0.0, AcquisCost);
    WriteValue(ListOut, 0, 0.0, 0.0, AcquisCost);

/* Count varies through the years of useful life for
    the item. For each year, depreciate the book value. */
    for (Count = 0; Count < (int) UsefulLife; Count++) {
        CurrentYr = (AcquisCost - ScrapValue) / UsefulLife;
        CumDeprec += CurrentYr;
        BookValue = AcquisCost - CumDeprec;
        StraightLn = (UsefulLife * UsefulLife + UsefulLife)
            / 2.0;
        WriteValue(stdout, Count + 1, CurrentYr, CumDeprec,
                BookValue);
        WriteValue(ListOut, Count + 1, CurrentYr, CumDeprec,
                BookValue);
    }
/* Do the sum-of-year's-digits analysis. Again print
    a banner, followed by the analysis. */
    WriteHeading(stdout, SUMYEARSDIGITS);
    WriteHeading(ListOut, SUMYEARSDIGITS);
    CumDeprec = 0.0;
    WriteValue(stdout, 0, 0.0, 0.0, AcquisCost);
    WriteValue(ListOut, 0, 0.0, 0.0, AcquisCost);

/* Count again varies over the years of life of the item. */
    for (Count = 0; Count < (int) UsefulLife; Count++) {
        YrsLeft = UsefulLife - Count;
        CurrentYr = YrsLeft / StraightLn *
            (AcquisCost - ScrapValue);
        CumDeprec += CurrentYr;
        BookValue = AcquisCost - CumDeprec;
        WriteValue(stdout, Count + 1, CurrentYr, CumDeprec,
                BookValue);
        WriteValue(ListOut, Count + 1, CurrentYr,
                CumDeprec, BookValue);
    }

/* Declining-balance analysis. Calculate the declining balance
    factor, and use this to control the number of years to
```

```
depreciate the item.  Note that Count stops when the book
value falls below the scrap value. */
WriteHeading(stdout, DECLINEBAL);
WriteHeading(ListOut, DECLINEBAL);
CumDeprec = 0.0;
DBFactor = (DBFactor / 100.0) / UsefulLife;
WriteValue(stdout, 0, 0.0, 0.0, AcquisCost);
WriteValue(ListOut, 0, 0.0, 0.0, AcquisCost);
CurrentYr = AcquisCost * DBFactor;
for (Count = 0;; Count++) {
    YrsLeft = UsefulLife - Count;
    CumDeprec += CurrentYr;
    BookValue = AcquisCost - CumDeprec;
    WriteValue(stdout, Count + 1, CurrentYr, CumDeprec,
            BookValue);
    WriteValue(ListOut, Count + 1, CurrentYr,
            CumDeprec, BookValue);
    CurrentYr = BookValue * DBFactor;
    if (BookValue < ScrapValue) {
        printf("\nCannot take depreciation below book value of:  %6.2f\n",
            ScrapValue);
        fprintf(ListOut,"\nCannot take depreciation below book value of:  %6.2f\n",
              ScrapValue);
              break;
        }
    }
}                                   /* main */

/* Collect the beginning values for all variables */
void StartingConditions() {       /* StartingConditions */

    Prompt("Type the name of the asset to be depreciated: ");
    fgets(ItemName, MAXSTRLEN, stdin);
    StripReturns(ItemName);
    printf("\nDescribe the asset -- %s:\n", ItemName);
    fgets(ItemDescr, MAXSTRLEN, stdin);
    StripReturns(ItemDescr);
    printf("\nGive the acquisition cost ($) of %s: ", ItemName);
    fflush(stdout);
    scanf("%f", &AcquisCost);
    Prompt("\nEnter the useful life in years: ");
    scanf("%d", &UsefulLife);
    printf("\nEstimate the salvage value at the end of %d years: ",
            UsefulLife);
    fflush(stdout);
    scanf("%f", &ScrapValue);
    Prompt("\nEnter the declining-balance factor (%): ");
    scanf("%f", &DBFactor);
}                                   /* StartingConditions */

/* WriteHeading prints a heading specific to the type of depreciation.
   WhichBanner is the control variable choosing the banner type.
   Demonstrate the use of the switch-case structure.*/
```

```
void WriteHeading(OutFile, WhichBanner)
int     WhichBanner;              /* Which banner to print */
FILE * OutFile;                   /* Target file */
{                                 /* WriteHeading */
    switch (WhichBanner) {
        case STRAIGHTLINE:
            fprintf(OutFile,"\n\n>>> STRAIGHT-LINE DEPRECIATION <<<\n\n");
            break;
        case SUMYEARSDIGITS:
            fprintf(OutFile,"\n\n>>> SUM-OF-YEARS-DIGITS DEPRECIATION <<<\n\n");
            break;

        case DECLINEBAL:
            fprintf(OutFile,"\n\n>>> DECLINING BALANCE DEPRECIATION: %3.0f%% FACTOR
            <<\n\n", DBFactor);
            break;
    } fprintf(OutFile,"       Current Year     Cumulative              Book\n");
    fprintf(OutFile,"Year   Depreciation     Depreciation            Value\n");
    fprintf(OutFile,"---------------------------------------------------------\n");
}                                 /* WriteHeading */

/* Write a banner to the printer describing the item. */
void WritePrinterBanner() {       /* WritePrinterBanner */
    WriteSolidLine(ListOut, 54, 0);
    fprintf(ListOut, "                  DEPRECIATION TABLES\n");
    WriteSolidLine(ListOut, 54, 0);
    fprintf(ListOut,"\nName of the Asset to Be Depreciated: %s\n", ItemName);
    fprintf(ListOut,"%s Is Described As:\n", ItemName);
    fprintf(ListOut," --> %s\n", ItemDescr);
    fprintf(ListOut,"Acquisition Cost ($): %9.2f\n", AcquisCost);
    fprintf(ListOut,"Useful Life of %s: %d Years.\n", ItemName, UsefulLife);
    fprintf(ListOut,"Scrap Value ($) at the End of %d Years: %7.2f\n\n",
        UsefulLife, ScrapValue);
}                                 /* WritePrinterBanner */

/* Print all depreciation lines to OutFile. */
void WriteValue(OutFile, YearNum, CurYr, Cumul, Book)
float   Book;                     /* Book value */
float   Cumul;                    /* Cumulative  */
float   CurYr;                    /* Current year */
FILE * OutFile;                   /* Target file to use */
int     YearNum;                  /* Which year */
{                                 /* WriteValue */
    fprintf(OutFile,"%2d      %10.2f      %10.2f      %10.2f\n",
        YearNum, CurYr, Cumul, Book);
}                                 /* WriteValue */
```

Give the Acquisition Cost ($) of ABC: **359.96**
Enter the Useful Life in Years: **5**
Estimate the Salvage Value at the End of 5.00 Years: **50**

Note that the program automatically inserted the asset's name and the number representing the useful life in years entered in the previous lines.

```
*******************************************************
                 DEPRECIATION TABLES
*******************************************************

Name of the Asset to Be Depreciated: ABC
ABC Is Described As:
 --> Dot-Matrix Printer with Serial Interface
Acquisition Cost ($):    359.96
Useful Life of ABC: 5 Years.
Scrap Value ($) at the End of 5 Years:   50.00


>>> STRAIGHT-LINE DEPRECIATION <<<

       Current Year       Cumulative             Book
Year   Depreciation       Depreciation           Value
-----------------------------------------------------
0            0.00              0.00             359.96
1           61.99             61.99             297.97
2           61.99            123.98             235.98
3           61.99            185.98             173.98
4           61.99            247.97             111.99
5           61.99            309.96              50.00

>>> SUM-OF-YEARS-DIGITS DEPRECIATION <<<

       Current Year       Cumulative             Book
Year   Depreciation       Depreciation           Value
-----------------------------------------------------
0            0.00              0.00             359.96
1          103.32            103.32             256.64
2           82.66            185.98             173.98
3           61.99            247.97             111.99
4           41.33            289.30              70.66
5           20.66            309.96              50.00

>>> DECLINING BALANCE DEPRECIATION: 200% FACTOR <<<

       Current Year       Cumulative             Book
Year   Depreciation       Depreciation           Value
-----------------------------------------------------
0            0.00              0.00             359.96
1          143.98            143.98             215.98
2           86.39            230.37             129.59
3           51.83            282.21              77.75
4           31.10            313.31              46.65

Cannot take depreciation below book value of:   50.00
```

Fig. 12-2. A sample of DEPREC3.

To enable the calculation of declining balance, the program asks for a percentage factor that will be applied to the straight line information:

Enter the Declining Balance Factor (%) : 200

As soon as we've entered the response to the last query, the computer starts to process the data. The screen begins to display the results of the calculations, and the printer begins the printed copy. All three methods, straight line, sum-of-years-digits, and declining balance are displayed on the screen while being printed. Your accountant can help you determine which of the methods (or another not shown here) is more advantageous to your situation.

Figure 12-2 is an actual printout the program generated for the data that we entered in the above example.

13

NETWORTH: Assets Calculation Program

Philosophically there are several ways to measure the worth of an individual. However, in the business community the measure of worth is made through quantitative calculations. This is especially true when one tries to establish a line of credit, make a loan, obtain a mortgage, or finance a purchase.

"What's your net worth?" is a question the prospective lender or creditor asks as he seeks data on which to base a decision about the borrower. It is also important to know your net worth in dollars in planning your estate, your will, or some investments.

Discovering your own net worth is a very simple arithmetic calculation. Total all your assets—those things you own that can be readily converted to cash—then total all your liabilities—all the cash you owe or are committed to pay out. Subtract the dollar amount of your liabilities from the amount of your assets:

Assets − Liabilities = Net Worth

The result of this short formula is what you are worth in pure dollars; what's left over after converting everything you own to cash and paying off all your debts. You may be surprised at how much (or how little) you are worth. (Please omit philosophy, humanity, and other non-materialistic concepts.)

You can determine your material progress by periodically measuring your net worth to keep track of its trend. Figure 13-1, NETWORTH, is designed to provide you with the discipline and the method for doing the calculations

Fig. 13-1. Source code for NETWORTH.

```
/* NETWORTH - COPYRIGHT 1986 by T. O. Sidebottom/L. A. Wortman     */

/*      Include Files
*/
#include <stdio.h>
#include <ctype.h>


/*      Definitions
*/
#define MAXASSET 17
#define MAXLIABILITIES 7
#define MAXSTRLEN 255
#define PRINTERNAME "prn"

/*      External declarations
*/
#include "utildefn.h"


/* Forward declarations
*/
void AsstWrapup();
void GetAssets();
void GetDebts();
void LiabWrapup();
void PrintInstructions();
void WrapUp();
void WriteBrokenLine();


/*      Global variables
*/
char   *AssetName[] = {          /* List of names of all assets */
    " Cash (Money On Hand)",
    " Savings Accounts",
    " Checking Accounts",
    " CD's",
    " Money Mart",
    " Stocks, Bonds",
    " Other Securities",
    " Notes Receivable",
    " Life Insurance Cash Value",
    " Rebates/Refunds Owed to You",
    " Vehicles",
    " Real Estate",
    " Annuities/Pensions",
    " Furniture/Appliances",
    " Jewelry/Cameras/Tools/Etc.",
    " Valuable Collections",
    " Other Assets"
};
```

```
char   *LiabName[] = {            /* List of names of all liabilities */
    " Contracts Outstanding",
    " Promissory Notes Payable",
    " Taxes Due and Unpaid",
    " Loans Outstanding",
    " Mortgages (Principal Amts)",
    " Court-Ordered Payments",
    " Other Debts"
};
FILE * ListOut;                   /* File opened to printer */
float   TotalAsset = 0.0;         /* Asset totals */
float   TotalLiab = 0.0;          /* Liability totals */

/*      Main program
*/
main(argc, argv)
int     argc;
char   *argv[];
{                                 /* main */
    char    Date[MAXSTRLEN];      /* Current date */
    char    Name[MAXSTRLEN];      /* User's name */

 /* Open the printer. If the open fails, stop the program. */
    if (!(ListOut = fopen(PRINTERNAME, "w"))) {
        fprintf(stderr, "Please check the printer. Is it on?");
        exit(1);
    }

 /* Print a login banner and instructions to the user. Then collect the
    user's name and the date. */
    SignOn("NETWORTH -- Personal Material Worth", 21, 50, 15);


    ClearScreen();
    printf("                          *** TURN ON THE PRINTER ***\n");
    WaitASecond();
    WaitASecond();
    ClearScreen();
    Prompt("Please type your full name: ");
    fgets(Name, MAXSTRLEN, stdin);
    Prompt("\nAnd the date of this statement (MM/DD/YY): ");
    fgets(Date, MAXSTRLEN, stdin);
    fprintf(ListOut, "%s", Name);
    fprintf(ListOut, "Personal Financial Statement\n");
    fprintf(ListOut, "as of: %s\n\n", Date);

 /* Processing consists of first listing instructions to the user, getting
    asset and debit information, and then listing the final report both to
    the display and to the printer. */
    PrintInstructions();
    GetAssets();
    GetDebts();
    WrapUp(stdout);
    WrapUp(ListOut);
 }                                /* main */
```

```
/* Prints the final asset report to OutFile */
void AsstWrapup(OutFile)
FILE * OutFile;                   /* Target output file */
{                                 /* AsstWrapup */
   WriteBrokenLine(OutFile);
   fprintf(OutFile,"TOTAL ASSETS:                     %10.2f\n", TotalAsset);
   WriteBrokenLine(OutFile);
}                                 /* AsstWrapup */

/* GetAssets asks to user to enter all assets. */
void GetAssets() {                /* GetAssets */
   int     AsstCtr;               /* Counter running through all assets */
   char    CheckChar[2];          /* Receives input characters from user */
   float   CurAsset;              /* Receives asset values from user */

 /* Print instructions to the user. */
   fprintf(ListOut, "ASSETS\n------\n");
   printf("\nThis Section Is For Your Assets......");
   printf("(Everything you own that has cash value.)\n\n");

 /* Loop through all assets. */
   for (AsstCtr = 0; AsstCtr < MAXASSET; AsstCtr++) {
   /* For each asset, print its name, and collect its value. */
      do {
         printf("\n %s: ", AssetName[AsstCtr]);
         fflush(stdout);
         scanf("%f", &CurAsset);

      /* Ask the user to validate input */
         Prompt("   Is the amount correct? (Y/N) ");
         scanf("%1s", CheckChar);
      } while (tolower(*CheckChar) != 'y');

   /* Accumulate total asset value. List value of this asset to the
      printer. */
      TotalAsset += CurAsset;
      fprintf(ListOut, "%30s %10.2f\n", AssetName[AsstCtr],
              CurAsset);
   }

 /* Print the final asset information to the screen and to the printer. */
   AsstWrapup(stdout);
   AsstWrapup(ListOut);
}                                 /* GetAssets */

/* Get debt information from the user. */
void GetDebts() {                 /* GetDebts */
   char    CheckChar;             /* Receives input characters from user */
   float   CurLiability;          /* Receives debt values from user */
   int     LiabCtr;               /* Counter running through all debts */

 /* Print instructions to the user. */
   printf("\n\n\nThis Section Is For Your Liabilities (Debts).\n\n");
   fprintf(ListOut, "\nLIABILITIES\n-----------\n");
```

```
   /* Loop through all liabilities. */
      for (LiabCtr = 0; LiabCtr < MAXLIABILITIES; LiabCtr++) {
   /* For each liability, print its name, and collect its value. */
       do {
           printf("\n %s: ", LiabName[LiabCtr]);
           fflush(stdout);
           scanf("%f", &CurLiability);

       /* Ask the user to validate input. */
           Prompt("   Is the amount correct? (Y/N) ");
           scanf("%1s", &CheckChar);
       } while (tolower(CheckChar) != 'y');
   /* Accumulate total liability value. List value of this liability to
      the printer. */
       TotalLiab += CurLiability;
       fprintf(ListOut, "%30s %10.2f\n", LiabName[LiabCtr],
               CurLiability);
   }

/* Print final liability information to the screen and to the printer. */
   LiabWrapup(stdout);
   LiabWrapup(ListOut);
}                                /* GetDebts */

/* Print the final liability report to OutFile */
void LiabWrapup(OutFile)
FILE * OutFile;                  /* Target output file */
{                                /* LiabWrapup */
    WriteBrokenLine(OutFile);
    fprintf(OutFile,
            "TOTAL LIABILITIES (DEBTS):     %10.2f\n", TotalLiab);
    WriteBrokenLine(OutFile);
    fprintf(OutFile, "\n");
}                                /* LiabWrapup */

/* Print instructions to the user. */
void PrintInstructions() {       /* PrintInstructions */
    printf("\n\nPlease enter amounts when requested.\n");
    printf("Do not enter commas.  Do enter decimal points.\n");
    printf("Respond 'Y' or 'N' when asked to confirm.\n");
    printf("Don't be concerned about errors.\n");
    printf("You will be able to correct them with 'N.'\n\n");
}                                /* PrintInstructions */

/* Print final net worth information. */
void WrapUp(OutFile)
FILE * OutFile;
{                                /* WrapUp */
    fprintf(OutFile, "\n");
    WriteSolidLine(OutFile, 41, 0);
    fprintf(OutFile, "\nNET WORTH:                        %10.2f\n\n",
            TotalAsset - TotalLiab);
```

```
    WriteSolidLine(OutFile, 41, 0);
}                                /* WrapUp */
/* Write a broken line to the target OutFile. */
void WriteBrokenLine(OutFile)
FILE * OutFile;                  /* Target file */
{                                /* WriteBrokenLine */
    fprintf(OutFile, "-=-=-=-=-=-=-=-=-=-=-=-=-=-=-=-=-=-=-=-=\n");
}                                /* WriteBrokenLine */
```

and generating a printed report of the results, ending with the dollar value of your net worth.

When you call the program by typing its name the screen displays a reminder to turn on the printer. As you run the program, the screen and the printer will respond at various times; therefore, the printer must be on from the very start.

Let's simulate a typical run, using a fictitious name and data. The first advisory message automatically scrolls off the screen and you are asked the first of a series of questions:

What is your name: **JONATHAN J. JONATHANBY**
What is the date of this statement? (MM/DD/YY) **10/30/86**

The screen scrolls the information up a few lines to make room for the following set of instructions:

Please enter amounts when requested.
Do not enter commas. Do enter decimal points.
Respond 'Y' or 'N' when asked to confirm.
Don't be concerned about errors.
You will be able to correct them with 'N.'

This section is for your assets . . .
(Everything you own that has cash value.)

Now the series of questions concerning assets begins. Here is a sample of the interaction with all responses to the questions shown in boldface:

Cash (Money On Hand): **550**
Is the amount correct? (Y/N)

You have an opportunity to change the dollars entered in response to the query about the amount of cash you have on hand. If you type N, your first response will be discarded by the program and the query will be repeated. If you type Y, the value you entered is stored and the next query appears on the screen:

```
JONATHAN J. JONATHANBY
Personal Financial Statement
as of: 10/30/86


ASSETS
------
             Cash (Money On Hand)     550.00
                 Savings Accounts   12505.59
                Checking Accounts     235.83
                             CD's    2000.00
                       Money Mart    1500.00
                    Stocks, Bonds    3100.00
                 Other Securities       0.00
                 Notes Receivable       0.00
        Life Insurance Cash Value   12354.00
      Rebates/Refunds Owed to You       0.00
                         Vehicles    6500.00
                      Real Estate   68000.00
              Annuities/Pensions        0.00
             Furniture/Appliances   12000.00
      Jewelry/Cameras/Tools/Etc.     2555.00
             Valuable Collections    1250.00
                     Other Assets       0.00
=-=-=-=-=-=-=-=-=-=-=-=-=-=-=-=-=-=-=-=-=-=
TOTAL ASSETS:                      122550.42
=-=-=-=-=-=-=-=-=-=-=-=-=-=-=-=-=-=-=-=-=-=

LIABILITIES
-----------
            Contracts Outstanding       0.00
        Promissory Notes Payable      300.00
             Taxes Due and Unpaid    1357.98
                Loans Outstanding    4005.00
      Mortgages (Principal Amts)    53478.72
           Court-Ordered Payments       0.00
                      Other Debts    2500.00
=-=-=-=-=-=-=-=-=-=-=-=-=-=-=-=-=-=-=-=-=-=
TOTAL LIABILITIES (DEBTS):          61641.70
=-=-=-=-=-=-=-=-=-=-=-=-=-=-=-=-=-=-=-=-=-=

*******************************************


NET WORTH:                          60908.72

*******************************************
```

Fig. 13-2. An actual report produced by NETWORTH.

Savings Account: **12505.59**
Is the amount correct? (Y/N) **Y**
Checking Account: **235.83**
Is the amount correct? (Y/N) **Y**

And so on, until all the questions about your money and your possessions have been answered in terms of dollars. At one point while making your ASSET entries, when the buffer has become full, the printer will start printing automatically. It does not query you at any point about a printed copy.

The screen displays the total of your assets and then continues with:

```
This Section Is For Your Liabilities (Debts).

Contracts Outstanding:  0
Is the amount correct? (Y/N)          Y

Promissory Notes Payable: 300
Is the amount correct? (Y/N)          N

Promissory Notes Payable: 500
Is the amount correct? (Y/N)          Y
```

As with the assets section, the queries about your liabilities continue until all facts have been revealed.

The total of the liabilities entries is calculated, displayed, and printed. Finally the two totals are subtracted from one another and the resulting number is displayed and printed with the label "NET WORTH." Thus, you have a complete, printed report you can file and save for comparison with your next progress check, or for presentation to your prospective lender or creditor. Figure 13-2 is a sample printout from this program.

14

ORDERLST: Sorting Alphanumeric Information

Often in both our business and personal worlds, it is desirable to alphabetize a list or rearrange information in numerical sequence. Data that is listed in a random fashion, without regard to the order of the letters of the alphabet, or not listed numerically in sequence from lowest to highest, is referred to as being *unordered*. The process of alphabetizing letters or words or of sequencing strings of numbers is referred to as *ordering*. Unordered information is listed at random. When information is in a sequential alphanumeric state, it is ordered or *sorted*.

The next program, ORDERLST, Fig. 14-1, accepts as its input a disk file of unordered information and generates an ordered file which is then automatically written to the disk, saved as a new file. The original, unordered file is not changed or removed, and retains the name by which it is identified in the disk's directory. The ordered list becomes a separate file, identified in the disk's directory by the name assigned to it when the ORDERLST program is called into action.

To illustrate the program at work, assume we have a file containing an unordered list of names and numbers. When the file was created and stored on disk we named it *messy*. That's the name by which the file is identified in the disk directory. The list is an ASCII file created with a text editor or word processor. We want to sort it out and create an ordered list without losing the original file.

Figure 14-2 is the content of the messy file. It's not a very long list. But it does demonstrate the action. ORDERLST can deal with many more lines

Fig. 14-1. Source code for ORDERLST.

```
/* ORDERLST - COPYRIGHT 1986 by T. O. Sidebottom/L. A. Wortman */

/*      Include Files
*/
#include <stdio.h>

/*      Definitions
*/
#define FALSE   0
#define MAXNUMLINES  1000
#define MAXSTRLEN 255
#define TRUE    1

/*      External declarations
*/
#include "utildefn.h"
extern char *malloc();

/* Forward declarations
*/
void SortBuffer();

/*      Global variables
*/
char    *Buffer[MAXNUMLINES];       /* Temporary buffer */
int      LineCnt;                   /* Current line count */

/*      Main program
*/
main(argc, argv)
int      argc;
char    *argv[];
{                                   /* main */
    int      Counter;               /* Loop variable */
    FILE * InFile;                  /* Input file */
    char     InLine[MAXSTRLEN];     /* Current input line */
    FILE * OutFile;                 /* Output file */
/* Open all files with three "arguments" on the command line.
   If too few arguments appear, or a file cannot be opened,
   stop the program, exiting gracefully to DOS. */
   if (argc < 3) {
       fprintf(stderr, "\nUsage: orderlst infilename outfilename.\n");
       exit(1);
   }
   if (!(InFile = fopen(argv[1], "r"))) {
       fprintf(stderr, "Can't open file %s.", argv[1]);
       exit(1);
   }
   if (!(OutFile = fopen(argv[2], "w"))) {
       fprintf(stderr, "Can't open file %s.", argv[2]);
       exit(1);
   }
```

```
 /* Read input line by line.  As we read the file, we store an
    image of it in memory. For each line, we allocate memory
    required to store the line using the function malloc.
    Note that we test to ensure malloc returns a valid value
    to us; if not, we're out of memory. */
    for (LineCnt = 0; LineCnt < MAXNUMLINES &&
            fgets(InLine, MAXSTRLEN, InFile); LineCnt++) {
        if (!(Buffer[LineCnt] = malloc(strlen(InLine) + 1))) {
            fprintf(stderr, "Insufficient memory to store file.");
            exit(1);
        }
        strcpy(Buffer[LineCnt], InLine);
    }

 /* Perform the sort */
    SortBuffer();

 /* List the sorted lines by looping through all valid lines. */
    for (Counter = 0; Counter < LineCnt; Counter++)
        fputs(Buffer[Counter], OutFile);
    fclose(InFile);
    fclose(OutFile);
}                                  /* main */

/* Sort the input lines */
void SortBuffer() {                /* SortBuffer */
    int     Counter;               /* Loop variable */
    int     HaveExchanged;         /* Set true if we've exchanged
                                      items on a particular sorting
                                      pass. The sort continues until
                                      we make a full pass through
                                      the list with this variable
                                      remaining FALSE. */
    char   *Temp;                  /* Temporary variable */

    do {
        HaveExchanged = FALSE;

    /* Loop through all elements and compare adjacent lines.
       If the lines are out of order, exchange the pointers
       to the lines. By exchanging the pointers, we don't
       recopy the entire lines, but just the memory
       addresses. */
        for (Counter = 1; Counter < LineCnt; Counter++)
            if (strcmp(Buffer[Counter], Buffer[Counter - 1]) < 0) {
            /* Exchange the two out-of-order entries. */
                HaveExchanged = TRUE;
                Temp = Buffer[Counter];
                Buffer[Counter] = Buffer[Counter - 1];
                Buffer[Counter - 1] = Temp;
            }
    /* Continue looping if we set HaveExchanged to
       TRUE during processing. */
    } while (HaveExchanged);
}                                  /* SortBuffer */
```

```
zebra
wortman
sidebottom
cantaloupe
antelope
barbarian
barnaby
total
yesterday
123
12ABC
years
yearling
yearly
sure
many
mostly
```

Fig. 14-2. MESSY, the file used to test ORDERLST's sorting capabilities.

of alphanumerics, and each line can be up to 255 characters in length.

To order this unordered list, we call upon our compiled program, ORDERLST. However, when we call ORDERLST at the command line, we must also call MESSY and assign a new name to the ordered list that will be generated. Let's call the new, ordered list *neat*, Fig. 14-3. Assume ORDERLST and MESSY are on the same disk. We also want NEAT to be on the same disk.

```
123
12ABC
antelope
barbarian
barnaby
cantaloupe
many
mostly
sidebottom
sure
total
wortman
yearling
yearly
years
yesterday
zebra
```

Fig. 14-3. NEAT, the sorted list produced by ORDERLST.

The procedure at the *command line* (the line where the system prompt is displayed) is as follows, in upper- or lowercase:

```
orderlst messy neat
```

The first filename is the program itself. The second filename is the unordered list, the one to be sorted or ordered. The third filename is the name we assign to the sorted or ordered list that will be created and written to the disk.

We can locate a file on one disk and write it to another merely by prefixing the letter or number (followed by a colon) of the drive on which the unordered file is located: conventional MS- and PC-DOS procedure. The same can be done with the ordered list that is generated: prefix the filename with the letter or number of the drive (followed by a colon) to which it is to be written. If you omit a drive identification, the computer will send the ordered file to the default drive, the one on which the ORDERLST program is located.

We can move the messy and neat files from drive to drive. For example, assume ORDERLST is on drive A and MESSY is on drive B. We want NEAT to appear on drive C. The command is:

```
orderlst b:messy c:neat
```

ORDERLST is the default drive A. MESSY is called from drive B. The prefixed drive identifier, c:, determines that NEAT will be stored on drive C. A prefix letter is not needed for NEAT if you want it to go to the default drive, A. If you wanted it to be written to drive B, you would have had to indicate this to the computer by prefixing the filename with the letter B and a colon. If you type the program's name, ORDERLST, on the command line and omit either or both of the required names, the screen will display a very straightforward instruction on the use of the command line, and make no changes in the files:

```
use: orderlst infilename outfilename
```

After ORDERLST has done its work, the file NEAT is the result of the response of the program to the correct input at the command line.

15

PERSREVU: Personnel Performance Review Program

"How am I doing, Boss?" This is the unspoken question of the majority of workers and managers who have a need to know how well they are performing in their jobs.

"Oh, how I'd like to tell you what I think of your work?" This is what may be going on in the mind of the supervisor with responsibility for the official performance evaluation or review of a subordinates' work. The implication is that there may be a communication problem between the superior and the subordinate in this scenario. To be valid and meaningful, performance reviews should be free of the influence of personal chemistry. As much as possible, they should be objective. However, it can be very difficult to separate objectivity from subjectivity and often impossible to prevent one from influencing the other.

PERSREVU, Fig. 15-1, presents a statistical approach to a performance review. The program asks eleven questions concerning the performance on the job of the person being reviewed. The questions can only be answered numerically, on a scale of 1 for the lowest to 5 for the highest level of performance.

The program totals the entries. The highest possible score is 55 (5 points for each of 11 entries). The lowest is 11 (1 point per entry). Scores below 11 and above 55 are rejected by the program as being a human error in typing the entries, and the review starts again from the top.

When a score between 11 and 55 has been obtained, the score is displayed without supporting detail. The screen invites you to make a printed copy, which contains the name of the person reviewed, the score for each of the eleven

Fig. 15-1. Source code for PERSREVU.

```
/* PERSREVU - COPYRIGHT 1986 by T. O. Sidebottom/L. A. Wortman  */

/* Include Files
*/
#include <stdio.h>
#include <ctype.h>

/*      Definitions
*/
#define FALSE   0
#define MAXSTRLEN 255
#define PRINTERNAME "prn"
#define TRUE    1

/*      External declarations
*/
#include "utildefn.h"

/* Forward declarations
*/
void GenerateReport();
void GetAppraisal();
void GetPrelimData();
void WriteGuideLines();

/*      Global variables
*/
int     Adaptability;           /* Person's adaptability score */
int     Attendance;             /* Person's attendance score */
int     Attitude;               /* Person's attitude score */
char    Date[MAXSTRLEN];        /* Current date */
char    Department[MAXSTRLEN];  /* Department name */
int     Dependability;          /* Dependability score */
int     Initiative;             /* Initiative score */
int     Knowledge;              /* Knowledge of the job score */
FILE * ListOut;                 /* File opened to the printer */
char    Name[MAXSTRLEN];        /* Person's name */
int     Personality;            /* Person's personality rating */
int     Potential;              /* Rating of person's potential */
int     Quality;                /* Rating of work quality */
int     Quantity;               /* Rating of work quantity */
int     Safety;                 /* Rating of job safety */
int     Score;                  /* Final score */
char    TestChar[2];            /* Receives input characters from user */

/*      Main program
*/
main() {                        /* main */

  /* Open the printer and list a banner to the display.
     If we can't open the printer, stop, go to DOS. */
     if (!(ListOut = fopen(PRINTERNAME, "w"))) {
```

```
        fprintf(stderr, "Can't open printer.");
        exit(1);
    }
    SignOn("PERSREVU -- Personnel Performance Review", 20, 50, 15);

/* This master loop repeats the review process for
   multiple employees until the user wants to stop */
    do {

    /* Clear the screen, and collect data. */
        ClearScreen();
        GetPrelimData();
        WriteGuideLines();
        GetAppraisal();

    /* The person's score is the sum of all 11 review factors. */
        Score = Quality + Knowledge + Quantity +
            Dependability + Initiative + Adaptability +
            Attitude + Attendance + Safety + Potential +
            Personality;

    /* An error trap for scores below 11. */
        if (Score < 11) {
            printf("The score for %s is below 11.\n\n", Name);
            printf("AN ERROR HAS BEEN FOUND. PLEASE REDO THE REVIEW.\n\n");
        /* Delay for about five seconds. */
            WaitFiveSeconds();
            TestChar[0] = 'y';
        }
    /* Here's a similar error trap for scores above 55. */
        else
            if (Score > 55) {
                printf("The score for %s is above 55.\n\n", Name);
                printf("AN ERROR HAS BEEN FOUND. PLEASE REDO THE REVIEW.\n\n");
            /* Delay for about five seconds. */
                WaitFiveSeconds();
                TestChar[0] = 'y';
            }
            else {
            /* Valid review score. Print review if the user desires. */
                printf("\n\n%s has a score of %d\n", Name, Score);
                Prompt("Do you want a detailed printout?  Y/N: ");
                scanf("%1s", TestChar);
                if (tolower(TestChar[0]) == 'y')
                    GenerateReport();

            /* See if the user wants another review. */
                Prompt("\nDo you want to do another review? (Y/N): ");
                scanf("%1s", TestChar);
            }
        if (tolower(TestChar[0]) != 'n')
            fgets(Name, MAXSTRLEN, stdin);
    } while (tolower(TestChar[0]) != 'n');
}                                   /* main */
```

```
 /* Print the final report, detailing all factors. */
 void GenerateReport() {          /* GenerateReport */

     WriteSolidLine(ListOut, 45.0);
     fprintf(ListOut, "Performance review of: %s\n", Name);
     fprintf(ListOut, "Department: %s\n", Department);
     fprintf(ListOut, "Reviewed on: %s\n", Date);
     WriteSolidLine(ListOut, 45, 0);
     fprintf(ListOut, "\n");

     fprintf(ListOut, "      Quality:        %d\n", Quality);
     fprintf(ListOut, "      Knowledge:      %d\n", Knowledge);
     fprintf(ListOut, "      Productivity:   %d\n", Quantity);
     fprintf(ListOut, "      Dependability:  %d\n", Dependability);
     fprintf(ListOut, "      Initiative:     %d\n", Initiative);
     fprintf(ListOut, "      Adaptability:   %d\n", Adaptability);
     fprintf(ListOut, "      Attitude:       %d\n", Attitude);
     fprintf(ListOut, "      Attendance:     %d\n", Attendance);
     fprintf(ListOut, "      Safety:         %d\n", Safety);
     fprintf(ListOut, "      Potential:      %d\n", Potential);
     fprintf(ListOut, "      Personality:    %d\n", Personality);

     fprintf(ListOut, "\nMaximum possible rating is 55.\n");
     fprintf(ListOut, "Minimum possible rating is 11.\n");
     fprintf(ListOut, "Mid-range rating is 33.\n");
     fprintf(ListOut, "Performance rating for %s is: %d\n", Name, Score)
     fprintf(ListOut, "%s", Name);
/* The following if-else loop tests for the value of Score and provides
   the appropriate response. */
   if (Score <= 13)
       fprintf(ListOut, " is a poor performer.\n\n");
   else
       if (Score <= 22)
           fprintf(ListOut, " just gets by.  Needs help.\n\n");
       else
           if (Score <= 43)
               fprintf(ListOut, " does acceptable work.\n\n");
           else
               if (Score <= 49)
                   fprintf(ListOut, " is a good performer.\n\n");
               else
                   fprintf(ListOut, " is exceptional.\n\n");

   WriteSolidLine(ListOut, 45, 0);
   fprintf(ListOut, "\nReviewer's initials: _________________\n");
   fprintf(ListOut, "\nDate of this review: _________________\n\n");
   WriteSolidLine(ListOut, 45, 0);
}                                 /* GenerateReport */

/* GetAppraisal collects the scores for the person being reviewed. */
void GetAppraisal() {             /* GetAppraisal */

 /* All collections happen by prompting the user, and using scanf
    to read the value entered. */
```

```
    printf("A - QUALITY\n");
    printf("  How well %s meets quality standards:       ", Name);
    fflush(stdout);
    scanf("%d", &Quality);

    printf("\nB - JOB KNOWLEDGE\n");
    printf("  Does %s understand all phases of the work? ", Name);
    fflush(stdout);
    scanf("%d", &Knowledge);

    printf("\nC - QUANTITY\n");
    Prompt("  Rate the productivity or output level:          ");
    scanf("%d", &Quantity);

    printf("\nD - DEPENDABILITY\n");
    printf("  Does %s follow instructions?                ", Name);
    fflush(stdout);
    scanf("%d", &Dependability);
    printf("\nE - INITIATIVE\n");
    printf("  Does %s originate constructive action?      ", Name);
    fflush(stdout);
    scanf("%d", &Initiative);

    printf("\nF - ADAPTABILITY\n");
    Prompt("  Ability to learn and adapt to changes:          ");
    scanf("%d", &Adaptability);

    printf("\nG - ATTITUDE\n");
    Prompt("  Willingness to cooperate and meet demands:      ");
    scanf("%d", &Attitude);

    printf("\nH - ATTENDANCE\n");
    Prompt("  Attendance and promptness:                      ");
    scanf("%d", &Attendance);

    printf("\nI - SAFETY AND ORDERLINESS\n");
    Prompt("  Compliance with rules for safety/housekeeping:  ");
    scanf("%d", &Safety);

    printf("\nJ - POTENTIAL FOR ADVANCEMENT\n");
    printf("  Rate leadership quality of %s:              ", Name);
    fflush(stdout);
    scanf("%d", &Potential);

    printf("\nK - PERSONALITY\n");
    Prompt("  Score ability to get along with others:         ");
    scanf("%d", &Personality);
}                              /* GetAppraisal */

/* Gets basic data about the person being reviewed. */
void GetPrelimData() {         /* GetPrelimData */
    Prompt("Name of the person being reviewed: ");
    fgets(Name, MAXSTRLEN, stdin);
 /* Because fgets stores the final newline with the string
```

```
    it reads, we use StripReturns to remove that character. */
    StripReturns(Name);

    Prompt("Department number or name:          ");
    fgets(Department, MAXSTRLEN, stdin);
    StripReturns(Department);

    Prompt("Date of this review (MM/DD/YY):     ");
    fgets(Date, MAXSTRLEN, stdin);
    StripReturns(Date);
    printf("\n\n");
}                                   /* GetPrelimData */

/* Write/display the instructions for the personnel review. */
void WriteGuideLines() {            /* WriteGuidelines */
    printf("You will evaluate %s for 11 factors.\n", Name);
    printf("The range for each factor is 1 (Min) to 5 (Max):\n\n");
    printf("     '1' is...............Poor performance.\n");
    printf("     '2' is...............Just gets by.\n");
    printf("     '3' is...............Acceptable.\n");
    printf("     '4' is...............Good.\n");
    printf("     '5' is...............Exceptional.\n\n");
    printf("You must rate each of the 11 factors.\n\n");
    printf("After you have rated the 11th factor, the\n");
    printf("result of the review will be displayed.\n\n\n");
}                                   /* WriteGuidelines */
```

characteristics, and a label (needs help, poor, acceptable, good, exceptional) for the quality of the work, as indicated by the score achieved. Also, space is provided on the printed copy for the reviewer's initials and the date of the review.

Here's a demonstration of the program, with our responses to the screen's questions shown in boldface:

> Type the name of the person being reviewed: **J. J. JANFERNWEIL**
> Department number or name: **Marketing. #23**
> Date of this review (MM/DD/YY): **08/15/86**

The program continues with a display of a set of instructions. Note that name "J. J. Janfernweil," a fictitious one used only for our example, is inserted into the instructions. This reminds the reviewer he or she is dealing with a specific person:

> You will evaluate J. J. Janfernweil for 11 factors.
> The range for each factor is 1 (Min) to 5 (Max):
>
> '1' is.................................Poor performance.
> '2' is.......................................Just gets by.
> '3' is..Acceptable.

'4' is . . . . Good.
'5' is . . . . Exceptional.
You must rate each of the 11 factors.
After you have rated the 11th factor, the
result of the review will be displayed.

Now the series of 11 factors begin to appear, each identified by a letter of the alphabet, from A-K:

A—QUALITY	
How well J. J. Janfernweil meets quality standards:	**4**
B—JOB KNOWLEDGE	
Does J. J. Janfernweil understand all phases of work?	**3**
C—QUANTITY	
Rate the productivity or output level:	**4**
D—DEPENDABILITY	
Does J. J. Janfernweil follow instructions?	**2**
E—INITIATIVE	
Does J. J. Janfernweil originate constructive action?	**3**
F—ADAPTABILITY	
Ability to learn and adapt to changes:	**2**
G—ATTITUDE	
Willingness to cooperate and meet demands:	**2**

```
Performance review of: J. J. FANFERNWEIL
Department: Marketing. #23
Reviewed on: 08/15/86
*********************************************

      Quality:        4
      Knowledge:      3
      Productivity:   4
      Dependability:  2
      Initiative:     3
      Adaptability:   2
      Attitude:       2
      Attendance:     4
      Safety:         3
      Potential:      2
      Personality:    2

Maximum possible rating is 55.
Minimum possible rating is 11.
Mid-range rating is 33.
Performance rating for J. J. FANFERNWEIL is: 31
J. J. FANFERNWEIL does acceptable work.

*********************************************

Reviewer's initials: ________________

Date of this review: ________________

*********************************************
```

Fig. 15-2. A sample report generated by PERSREVU.

H—ATTENDANCE

Attendance and promptness:	**4**

I—SAFETY AND ORDERLINESS

Compliance with rules for safety/housekeeping:	**3**

J—POTENTIAL FOR ADVANCEMENT

Rate leadership quality of J. J. Janfernweil:	**2**

K—PERSONALITY

Score ability to get along with others:	**2**

As soon as you type the score for item K and press the Enter key, the screen displays the tally:

J. J. Janfernweil has a score of 31
Do you want a detailed printout? Y/N: **Y**

By typing the letter Y you instruct the program to send the data to the printer. The complete printout produced by the program on the basis of the information entered above is shown in Fig. 15-2.

The full evaluation of the data, the determination of corrective courses of action that might be planned and implemented to reinforce J. J. Janfernweil's weaknesses (as indicated by the computer's calculations and responses) are for the reviewer and his aides to determine. Within the limitations and restraints of prejudices and halo effects, the PERSREVU program has supplied relatively objective values concerning strengths and weaknesses. At this point, humans must take charge.

16

PLOTTER: Plotting Equally Spaced Data on X-Y Axes

This program makes it possible to use most printers, with or without a graphics capability, to generate a complete display of data points plotted on X and Y axes. As with all programs in this book, PLOTTER, Fig. 16-1, is highly interactive. The data points are represented by the letter x (or, by means of a simple change you can make in the source code, any other character of your choice) and are completely enclosed in a box-like set of axes with calibration points that are automatically set by the program.

The first message displayed on the screen is the important advice to turn on the printer. The "width" of the graph is actually the Y axis, the height of the completed graph when the printout is properly oriented. ("Properly oriented" simply means turn the printed sheet 90-degrees counter-clockwise, thereby setting the Y axis at the left side.) The Y axis is automatically calibrated according to the number you enter as the width in inches. This means the highest calibrated point of the printed graph's height will be the same as the number entered as width.

The limitation on width (or final height) is the width of the screen in number of columns (80) divided by the number of characters per inch (10). However, in order to avoid wrap-around on the axes, the maximum usable width is 7.5 inches.

Because the Y-axis is self-calibrating, the largest data value you enter will determine the locations of the data points in the graph. The recommended way to determine the width is to make the width equal to the largest data value

Fig. 16-1. Source code for PLOTTER.

```
/* PLOTTER - COPYRIGHT 1986 by T. O. Sidebottom/L. A. Wortman */

/*      Include Files
*/
#include <stdio.h>
#include <ctype.h>

/*      Definitions
*/
#define FALSE   0
#define MAXNUMPOINTS  50
#define MAXSTRLEN 255
#define PRINTERNAME "prn"
#define TRUE    1

/*      External declarations
*/
#include "utildefn.h"

/* Forward declarations
*/
void WriteGraph() ;

/*      Code macros
*/
#define Max(a,b)        ((a > b) ? a : b)
#define Min(a,b)        ((a < b) ? a : b)

/* Forward declarations
*/
void PrintGrafStat();
void WriteAxis();
void WriteSpaces();

/*      Global variables
*/
float   Factor;                 /* Scaling factor */
float   Greatest = 0.0;         /* Value of largest input data */
int     NumPoints;              /* Number of points to plot */
float   Points[MAXNUMPOINTS];   /* Values to plot */
float   TensWidth;              /* Width multiplied by ten */
int     Width;                  /* Requested width */

/*      Main program
*/
main(argc, argv)
int     argc;
char    *argv[];
{                               /* main */
    int     Counter;            /* Loop variable */
    FILE * ListOut;             /* File opened to printer */
    char    TestChar;           /* Receives characters from user */
```

```
/* Open the printer. If we fail, stop. */
   if (!(ListOut = fopen(PRINTERNAME, "w"))) {
       fprintf(stderr, "Can't open printer.");
       exit(1);
   }

/* Print a startup banner on the display. */
   SignOn("PLOTTER -- Data Plots On X-Y Axes", 23, 50, 15);

/* Get basic information about the graph size and number of
   plotted points */
   ClearScreen();
   Prompt(
      "Type the WIDTH in INCHES for the GRAPH to be Plotted: ");
   scanf("%d", &Width);
   Prompt(
      "What is the Number of Points to Be Plotted? (50 Max):  ");
   scanf("%d", &NumPoints);

/* Number of points to plot is the minimum of the number the
   user entered and the maximum number we can plot. */
   NumPoints = Min(NumPoints, MAXNUMPOINTS);

/* Collect the actual values by looping through the entire
   array, and prompting the user for input. */
   printf("\n(Do NOT type Negative Values.)\n");
   fprintf(ListOut, "Values Are:\n");
   for (Counter = 0; Counter < NumPoints; Counter++) {
       printf("Type the value for point %d: ", Counter + 1);
       fflush(stdout);
       scanf("%f", &Points[Counter]);
       fprintf(ListOut, "%12.4f\n", Points[Counter]);
   }
/* Find the scaling factor by finding the largest value in the list.
   Then print statistics we derived from the scaling process. */
   TensWidth = Width * 10;
   for (Counter = 0; Counter < NumPoints; Counter++)
       Greatest = Max(Greatest, Points[Counter]);
   Factor = TensWidth / Greatest;
   PrintGrafStat(stdout);
   PrintGrafStat(ListOut);

/* Print the graph on the display and on the printer. Optionally
   let the user make multiple graphs. */
   do {
       WriteGraph(stdout);
       WriteGraph(ListOut);
   /* Flush the contents of the buffer; finish the printout */
       fflush(ListOut);
   /* Send a formfeed to the printer and sound the bell */
       fprintf(ListOut,"\f\7");
   /* Send a query for the user to see at the screen */
       Prompt("\nRepeat the printout of the graph? ('Y' or 'N'): ");
       scanf("%1s", &TestChar);
```

```
    } while (tolower(TestChar) != 'n');
}                               /* main */

/* Write statistics about the plot to OutFile.
 */
void PrintGrafStat(OutFile)
FILE * OutFile;                 /* Target file */
{                               /* PrintGrafStat */
    fprintf(OutFile,
            "\nMaximum Value: %12.4f\n", Greatest);
    fprintf(OutFile,
            "Value at the Top of the Graph: %12.4f\n",
            Greatest);
    fprintf(OutFile,
            "The Graph is %d Inches Wide (at 10 CPI).\n\n",
            Width);
}                               /* PrintGrafStat */

/* Print the axis to the target output file */
void WriteAxis(OutFile)
FILE * OutFile;                 /* Target file */
{                               /* WriteAxis */
    int     Counter;            /* Loop variable */

    for (Counter = 0; Counter < (int) (TensWidth / 5); Counter++)
        fprintf(OutFile, "+----");
    fprintf(OutFile, "+\n");
}                               /* WriteAxis */

/* Print the actual graph to the output file */
void WriteGraph(OutFile)
FILE * OutFile;                 /* Target file */
{                               /* WriteGraph */
    int     Counter;            /* Loop variable */
    int     NumSpaces;          /* Number of spaces to move over */
    int     PointCount;         /* Loops through each point */

    fprintf(OutFile, "\n\n");
    WriteAxis(OutFile);

 /* Loop through all points */
    for (PointCount = 0; PointCount < NumPoints; PointCount++) {

    /* Loop through all columns to print. */
        for (Counter = 0;
             Counter < (int) (0.5 * TensWidth / NumPoints); Counter++) {
            fprintf(OutFile, ":");
            WriteSpaces(OutFile, (int) (TensWidth - 1));
            fprintf(OutFile, ":\n");
        }
        NumSpaces = (int) (Factor * Points[PointCount]);
        if (NumSpaces == 0) {
        /* Point at the beginning of the graph. */
            fprintf(OutFile, "*");
            WriteSpaces(OutFile, (int) (TensWidth - 1));
```

```
            fprintf(OutFile, ":\n");
        }
        else
            if (NumSpaces == (int) TensWidth) {
                fprintf(OutFile, ":");
                WriteSpaces(OutFile, (int) (TensWidth - 1));
                fprintf(OutFile, "x\n");
            }
            else {
                fprintf(OutFile, ":");
                WriteSpaces(OutFile, NumSpaces - 1);
                fprintf(OutFile, "x");
                WriteSpaces(OutFile, (int) (TensWidth - 1 - NumSpaces));
                fprintf(OutFile, ":\n");
            }
    }
    WriteAxis(OutFile);
}                               /* WriteGraph */

/* Write specified number of spaces to the output file */
void WriteSpaces(OutFile, Num)
int     Num;                    /* Number of spaces to write */
FILE * OutFile;                 /* Target File */
{                               /* WriteSpaces */
    int     Counter;            /* Loop variable */

    for (Counter = 0; Counter < Num; Counter++)
        fprintf(OutFile, " ");
}                               /* WriteSpaces */
```

you want represented on thc graph. Thc largest data value should be expressed as a single-digit integer of this value. For example, if you want to enter a maximum data point value for 54321.85, the width of the graph should be set at 5. This is the value used in our example. In our sample run, our responses to the questions are shown in boldface:

Type the WIDTH in INCHES for the GRAPH to be Plotted: **5**

The next query is:

What is the Number of Points to Be Plotted? (50 Max): **10**

The screen advises:

Do NOT Type Negative Values.

Then the data values are entered from the keyboard, as in this example:

Type the Value for Point 1: **1.12**
Type the Value for Point 2: **4.34**

```
Values Are:
      1.1200        2.7500
      4.3400        1.9500
      3.3300        5.4300
      3.0000        4.7500
      3.9500        3.5000


Maximum Value:       5.4300
Value at the Top of the Graph:       5.4300
The Graph is 5 Inches Wide (at 10 CPI).
+----+----+----+----+----+----+----+----+----+----+
:                                                 :
:                                                 :
:         x                                       :
:                                                 :
:                                                 :
:                                      x          :
:                                                 :
:                                                 :
:                             x                   :
:                                                 :
:                                                 :
:                          x                      :
:                                                 :
:                                                 :
:                                   x             :
:                                                 :
:                                                 :
:                        x                        :
:                                                 :
:                                                 :
:                x                                :
:                                                 :
:                                                 :
:                                                x:
:                                                 :
:                                                 :
:                                          x      :
:                                                 :
:                                                 :
:                               x                 :
+----+----+----+----+----+----+----+----+----+----+
```

Fig. 16-2. The raw data plot created by a run of PLOTTER.

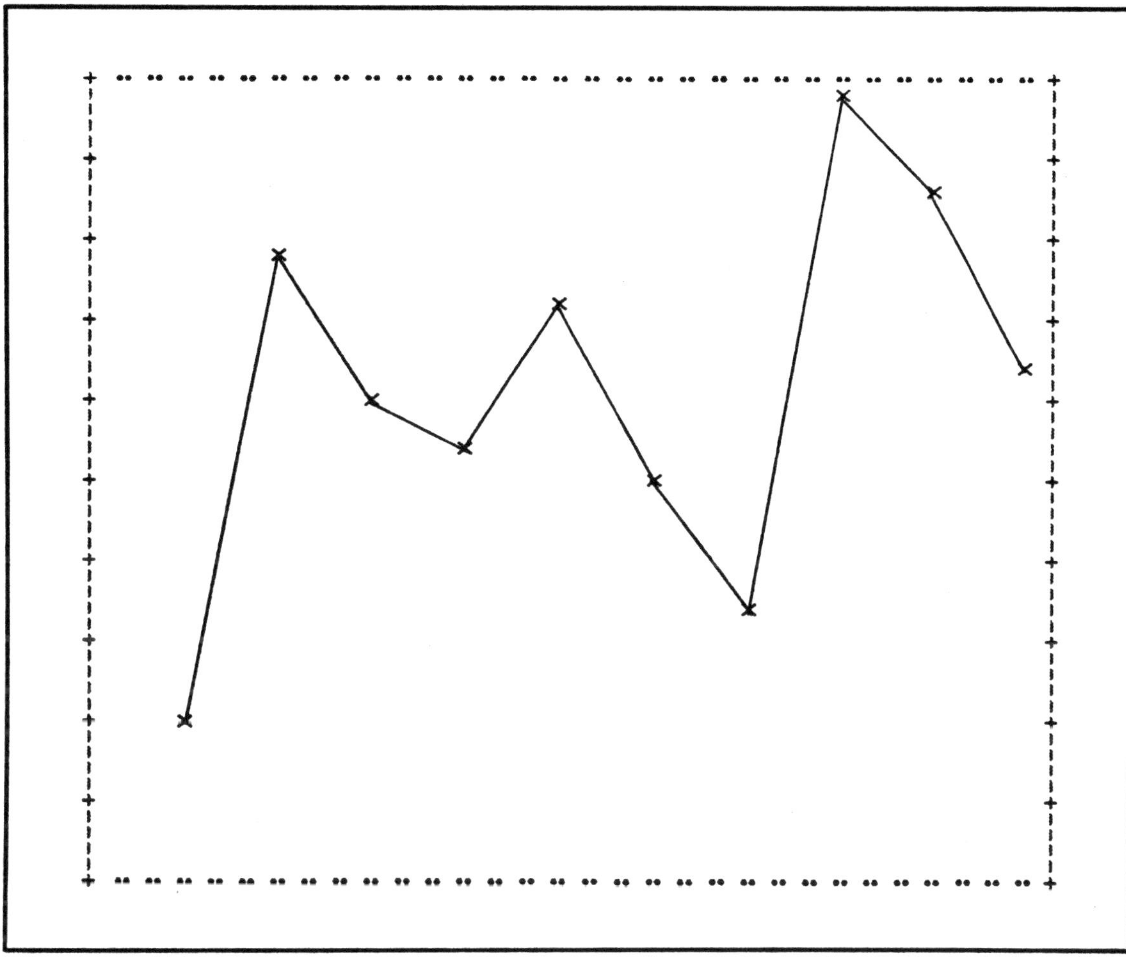

Fig. 16-3. The data plot with the points connected and properly oriented.

Type the Value for Point 3: **3.33**
Type the Value for Point 4: **3.00**
Type the Value for Point 5: **3.95**
Type the Value for Point 6: **2.75**
Type the Value for Point 7: **1.95**
Type the Value for Point 8: **5.43**
Type the Value for Point 9: **4.75**
Type the Value for Point 10: **3.50**

When the last entry has been made and the enter key has been pressed, the following summarizing information is displayed:

Maximum Value: 5.43
Value at the Top of the Graph: 5.43
The Graph is 5.00 Inches Wide (at 10 CPI).

Then the printer automatically goes to work. The ten data values that have been entered are listed and the graph is printed. Figure 16-2 is a sample printout.

Use a straight-edge to link the data points (represented by the character "x" in our example) and you have the finished product, as in Fig. 16-3.

17

PROFCON: Profit Contribution Analysis Program

Nonprofit organization's employees can skip this chapter—unless they want to see how some aspects of profitability can be calculated by a computer. There are a number of factors that determine whether a product or a service is making a quantifiable contribution to the profitability of the company. Our next program, PROFCON, (Fig. 17-1), delineates those factors and their measurable effects.

To make PROFCON perform its functions, you have to know several things about the product or the service the company is selling. A run-through of the program demonstrates what you must know.

The program signs on, displaying a banner on the screen:

```
****************************
 Profit Contribution Analysis
****************************
```

After approximately one second, the banner scrolls off the screen and the first of a series of questions is asked. (Our responses to the questions are shown in bold):

What is the name or model of the unit?	**EasyCome**
What is the selling price per EasyCome?	**34.95**
What is the cost of materials per unit?	**4.57**

Fig. 17-1. Source code for PROFCON.

```
/* PROFCON - COPYRIGHT 1986 by T. O. Sidebottom/L. A. Wortman  */

/*      Include Files
*/
#include <stdio.h>

/*      Definitions
*/
#define MAXSTRLEN 255

/*      Main program
*/
main(argc, argv)
int     argc;
char    *argv[];
{                               /* main */
    char    CheckChar;          /* Receives characters from user */
    float   Commission;         /* Commission amount */
    float   DirLabor;           /* Direct labor cost */
    float   Materials;          /* Materials cost */
    float   Misc;               /* Miscellaneous cost */
    char    Name[MAXSTRLEN];    /* Unit name */
    float   Royalties;          /* Royalties cost */
    float   SellPrice;          /* Selling price */
    float   ShipCost;           /* Shipping cost */
    float   Sum;                /* Sum of values */

 /* Print startup banner. */
    SignOn("PROFCON -- Profit Contribution Report", 20, 50, 15);

    do {
    /* Clear the screen and get the data to be analyzed. */
        ClearScreen();
        Prompt("Name or Model of the Item:      ");
        scanf("%s", Name);
        printf("\nSelling Price Per %s:  ", Name);
        fflush(stdout);
        scanf("%f", &SellPrice);
        Prompt("\nCost of Materials Per Unit:   ");
        scanf("%f", &Materials);
        Prompt("\nDirect Labor Cost Per Unit:   ");
        scanf("%f", &DirLabor);
        Prompt("\nShipping Cost Per Unit:       ");
        scanf("%f", &ShipCost);
        Prompt("\nCommission ($) Paid Per Unit: ");
        scanf("%f", &Commission);
        Prompt("\nRoyalties Paid Per Unit:      ");
        scanf("%f", &Royalties);
        Prompt("\nMiscellaneous Direct Costs:   ");
        scanf("%f", &Misc);
        ClearScreen();
```

```
    /* Print the report to the user's display (stdout). */
       WriteSolidLine(stdout, 59, 0);
       printf("          %s -- Contribution Analysis\n", Name);
       WriteSolidLine(stdout, 59, 0);
       printf("\nSelling Price Per Unit:                  %10.2f\n",
              SellPrice);
       printf("\nLess the Variable Costs:\n");
       printf(" Materials:       %10.2f\n", Materials);
       printf(" Direct Labor:    %10.2f\n", DirLabor);
       printf(" Shipping:        %10.2f\n", ShipCost);
       printf(" Commission:      %10.2f\n", Commission);
       printf(" Royalties:       %10.2f\n", Royalties);
       printf(" Misc. Costs:     %10.2f\n\n", Misc);
       Sum = Materials + DirLabor + ShipCost + Commission +
           Royalties + Misc;
       printf("Total Variable Costs:                    %10.2f\n\n",
              Sum);
       printf("Unit Contribution to Profit:             %10.2f\n\n",
              SellPrice - Sum);

    /* Ask if the user wants to do another analysis. */
       Prompt("Do another calculation? (Y/N): ");
       scanf("%1s", &CheckChar);
    }
  /* If the user enters 'n' or 'N', exit the program. */
    while (CheckChar != 'n' && CheckChar != 'N');
}                                /* main */
```

What is the direct labor cost per unit?	**2.43**
What is the shipping cost per unit?	**1.29**
What commission-dollars are paid per unit?	**1.75**
What royalties are paid per unit?	**.50**
Enter any miscellaneous direct costs:	**.50**

As soon as you have entered the last figure and have pressed the enter key, the screen clears and the results of the calculations are displayed under a banner that contains the name or model of the product (or service) that is being analyzed. See Fig. 17-2 for the results of this program.

The contribution to profit is the selling price minus the total variable costs. Indirect, overhead and administrative costs are not used in this calculation. The positive $23.91 per unit must support these costs and meet the company's target profit-margin.

By running PROFCON for various products and services, the relative contributions to profit can be determined and compared, and the probability for success associated with decision-making can become greater. The screen asks the question:

Do another calculation? Y/N:

```
************************************************
          EasyCome -- Contribution Analysis
************************************************
Selling price per unit:                    34.95
Less the variable costs:
 Materials:                      4.57
 Direct Labor:                   2.43
 Shipping:                       1.29
 Commission:                     1.75
 Royalties:                      0.50
 Misc. Costs:                    0.50
Total variable costs:                      11.04
Unit contribution to profit:               23.91
************************************************
```

Fig. 17-2. Display of the computed results of a run of PROFCON.

If you enter an N response the PROFCON program ends at once.

No provision has been made in the code for sending the calculations to the printer. As an interesting exercise, borrow the appropriate sections of code from other programs in this book. In this way you may write the code to send the results to the printer or, if you prefer, use the Shift-PrtSc capability of the IBM PC or XT.

18

REPCOM: Sales Representative Commission Reporter

Every marketing and sales manager deals with numbers. "They come with the territory," is the old saying. The numbers may represent units, dollars, forecasts, quotas, variances, discounts, mark-ups, salaries, spiffs, commissions, incentives, bonuses, and expenses. The expression "sales manager arithmetic" covers the whole range of numeric data with which the sales manager is concerned and with which the manager must work every day.

Sales manager arithmetic includes the very important payment of commissions to sales representatives or agents. What is the total dollar volume of orders (or sales, depending on the basis for calculations) for which the reps or agents are to be commissioned? What is the commission rate in percent? (The rate often differs from product to product, and may differ from rep to rep.) How much has each rep or agent earned in dollars? How much has been paid out against the earned amount? How much is still owed to each?

Then, what is the total amount of all sales achieved? What is the total amount that has been paid to date for all reps or agents? And what is the total amount still owed, but not yet paid? Not very complex arithmetic; however, if done manually, the calculations can be time-consuming and tiresome. Such projects are, by their very nature, subject to outrageous human errors.

This essential bundle of information can be assembled, calculated, and an accurate report printed out in a jiffy with the REPCOM program, Fig. 18-1. When you call for REPCOM, the program signs on with an identifying banner. This banner scrolls off the screen to reveal the first question. Our responses to the questions are shown in bold:

Fig. 18-1. Source code for REPCOM.

```
/* REPCOM - COPYRIGHT 1986 by T. O. Sidebottom/L. A. Wortman  */

/*      Include Files
*/
#include <stdio.h>

/*      Definitions
*/
#define FALSE   0
#define MAXNUMREPS 25
#define MAXSTRLEN 255
#define PRINTERNAME "prn"
#define TRUE    1

/* Forward declarations
*/
void WrapUp();
void WriteRepReport();

/*      Global variables
*/
char    Date[MAXSTRLEN];           /* Current date */
FILE * ListOut;                    /* File opened to printer */
int     RepNum = 0;                /* Representative number */
float   RepCommDue;                /* Commission due to representative */
float   RepCommEarn;               /* Commission earned */
float   RepCommPaid;               /* Commission paid */
float   RepCommRate;               /* Commission rate */
float   RepVolume;                 /* Volume for representative */
float   TotCommDue = 0.0;          /* Total commission due */
float   TotCommEarn = 0.0;         /* Total commission earned */
float   TotCommPaid = 0.0;         /* Total commission paid */
float   TotalSales = 0.0;          /* Total sales */
/*      Main program
*/
main() {                           /* main */

 /* Open the printer. If we can't open it, stop. */
    if (!(ListOut = fopen(PRINTERNAME, "w"))) {
        fprintf(stderr, "Can't talk to the printer. Is it on?");
        exit(1);
    }

 /* Print a login banner and prompt for basic information
    about the report. */
    SignOn(
     "REPCOM -- Sales Rep's Commission Report", 20, 50, 15);

    Prompt("What is the date of this report? (MM/DD/YY): ");
    fgets(Date, MAXSTRLEN, stdin);
    WriteSolidLine(ListOut, 40, 0);
    fprintf(ListOut,"\n  STATUS OF COMMISSIONS AS OF: %s\n", Date);
```

```
   WriteSolidLine(ListOut, 40, 0);
   fprintf(ListOut, "\n");

/* Display instructions for the user. */
   printf("\n\nEnter the SALES VOLUME for each Rep when prompted.\n");
   printf("When all entries are completed, type -1 in response\n");
   printf("to the next request for 'Sales Volume.'\n\n\n");

/* Continue collecting information until the user enters a -1. */
   do {

   /* Get the beginning sales volume. If the user enters a
      negative number, skip all other input queries. */
       printf("Enter the Sales Volume for Rep %d: ", RepNum + 1);
       fflush(stdout);
       scanf("%f", &RepVolume);

       if (RepVolume >= 0) {
       /* Collect all information about this representative. */
           printf("Enter the Commission-Rate (%%): ");
           fflush(stdout);
           scanf("%f", &RepCommRate);
           RepCommEarn = RepVolume * (RepCommRate / 100.0);
           printf("Commissions Earned: %10.2f\n", RepCommEarn);
           printf("Enter the Commissions Paid to Rep %2d: ", RepNum + 1);
           fflush(stdout);
           scanf("%f", &RepCommPaid);
           RepCommDue = RepCommEarn - RepCommPaid;
           printf("Commissions Still Unpaid: %10.2f\n\n", RepCommDue);
           WriteRepReport();
           TotalSales += RepVolume;
           TotCommEarn += RepCommEarn;
           TotCommPaid += RepCommPaid;
           TotCommDue += RepCommDue;
           RepNum++;
       }
   } while (RepVolume >= 0);
   printf("\n");

/* Print the final report to the display and to the printer. */
   WrapUp(stdout);
   WrapUp(ListOut);
}                              /* main */

/* Send a wrapup of the data to the output file. */
void WrapUp(OutFile)
FILE * OutFile;                /* Target file */
{                              /* WrapUp */
   WriteSolidLine(OutFile, 40, 0);
   fprintf(OutFile, "Total Sales for All Reps:    %13.2f\n", TotalSales);
   fprintf(OutFile, "Total Commissions Earned:    %13.2f\n", TotCommEarn);
   fprintf(OutFile, "Total Commissions Paid:      %13.2f\n", TotCommPaid);
   fprintf(OutFile, "Total Commissions Unpaid:    %13.2f\n", TotCommDue);
   WriteSolidLine(OutFile, 40, 0);
}                              /* WrapUp */
```

```
/* Print information about each representative. */
void WriteRepReport() {          /* WriteRepReport */
    fprintf(ListOut, "\n---------- Report for Rep %d ------------\n\n", RepNum + 1);
    fprintf(ListOut, "Sales Volume:                %12.2f\n", RepVolume);
    fprintf(ListOut, "Commission Rate: %6.2f%%\n", RepCommRate);
    fprintf(ListOut, "Commissions Earned:          %12.2f\n", RepCommEarn);
    fprintf(ListOut, "Commissions Paid:            %12.2f\n", RepCommPaid);
    fprintf(ListOut, "Commissions Unpaid:          %12.2f\n\n\n", RepCommDue);
}                                /* WriteRepReport */
```

What Is the Date of this Report? (MM/DD/YY): **09/15/86**

Then instructions are displayed on the screen:

Enter the SALES VOLUME for each Rep when prompted.
When all entries are completed, type −1 in response
to the next request for 'Sales Volume.'
Enter the Sales Volume for Rep 1: **12345.67**
Enter the Commission-Rate (%): **12.5**

The computer instantly calculates and displays the dollars earned in commissions:

Commissions Earned: 1543.21

The computer then asks you to:

Enter the Commissions Paid to Rep 1: **1000**

and displays dollar amount still owed to the Rep:

Commissions Still Unpaid: 543.21

The program continues:

Enter the Sales Volume for Rep 2: **23456.78**
Enter the Commission Rate (%): **15**

Commissions Earned: **3518.52**
Enter the Commissions Paid to Rep 2: **3000**
Commissions Still Unpaid: **518.52**
Enter the Sales Volume for Rep 3: **−1**

To illustrate the final printed copy, we deliberately ended the report after completing the data for Rep 2 by entering −1 when the instruction appears to "Enter the Sales Volume for Rep 3: ." The program could have been continued,

```
*****************************************
  STATUS OF COMMISSIONS AS OF: 09/15/86

*****************************************


---------- Report for Rep 1 ------------

Sales Volume:                   12345.67
Commission Rate:  12.50%
Commissions Earned:              1543.21
Commissions Paid:                1000.00
Commissions Unpaid:               543.21



---------- Report for Rep 2 ------------

Sales Volume:                   23456.78
Commission Rate:  15.00%
Commissions Earned:              3518.52
Commissions Paid:                3000.00
Commissions Unpaid:               518.52


*****************************************
Total Sales for All Reps:       35802.45
Total Commissions Earned:        5061.73
Total Commissions Paid:          4000.00
Total Commissions Unpaid:        1061.73
*****************************************
```

Fig. 18-2. Report generated by REPCOM.

detailing the information for up to 25 reps or sales agents. The maximum number of reps or sales agents can be increased or decreased by changing the number in the definition shown in the source code as:

```
#define MAXNUMREPS 25
```

Figure 18-2 is the final report, exactly as it was printed automatically when −1 was entered for Sales Volume to signal the end of the entries.

19

SALESPWR: Sales Performance Analyzer and Report Writer

Salespeople, products, markets, agents, distributors, wholesalers and retailers are all involved in quantitative and measurable activities. When the objective is sales, it's easy to determine whether or not sales are being made. Simple—isn't it?

Sometimes variables are involved that cloud the issue, such as when quotas are not being made and shipments and cash flow fall off, or when quotas are being exceeded and the company is not prepared for the unforecasted demand. In the latter case there may be a sudden scramble for additional resources of money, materials, labor, and facilities in an effort to respond to and capitalize on the unexpected inflow of orders.

Even in good times, when the aggregate of all sales meets the total budget, it's important to know which people, customers, markets, products or services are responsible for the bounty. In all cases, regardless of who or what is being measured, it is important to gather facts for analysis and decision-making. In the sales environment "facts" include specific data concerning: sales volume by individual, account, market, or product; total combined sales volume; average sales volume; who or what is above the average, and by what amount; who or what is below the average, and by what amount.

SALESPWR, Fig. 19-1, is designed to analyze this information, becoming a time-saver as a calculator and report writer. The SALESPWR program accepts up to 51 entries, which should be more than enough for most situations. Counting the entries (record numbers) is automatic, advancing by one after each new entry is made. A record can be a person, market, company, customer, or product. The key to the record numbers should be kept apart

Fig. 19-1. Source code for SALESPWR.

```
/* SALESPWR - COPYRIGHT 1986 by T. O. Sidebottom/L. A. Wortman */

/*      Include Files
*/
#include <stdio.h>
#include <ctype.h>

/*      Definitions
*/
#define MAXNUMIDS       51
#define MAXSTRLEN       255
#define PRINTERNAME     "prn"

/*      External declarations
*/
#include "utildefn.h"

/* Forward declarations
*/
void GenerateReport();
void StartingConditions();

/*      Global variables
*/
float   AvgSales;               /* Average sales for period */
char    EndDate[MAXSTRLEN];     /* Ending date for period */
FILE * ListOut;                 /* File opened to printer */
int     NumIds = 0;             /* Number of items to process */
float   SalesAmt[MAXNUMIDS];    /* Sales amount for each item */
char    StartDate[MAXSTRLEN];   /* Starting date for period */
char    TodaysDate[MAXSTRLEN];  /* Today's date */
float   TotalSales = 0.0;       /* Total sales for period */

/*      Main program
*/
main(argc, argv)
int     argc;
char   *argv[];
{                               /* main */
    char    TestChar;           /* Receives character input from user */
 /* Print signon banner. Retrieve starting information. */
    SignOn("SALESPWR -- Sales Power Report", 24, 50, 15);

    StartingConditions();
    WaitASecond();
    ClearScreen();

 /* Display the report on the screen. */
    GenerateReport(stdout);

 /* Optionally print a report on the printer. */
    printf("\n\nPrintout? Turn on the printer, please.");
```

```
    Prompt(" Then, type 'Y' or 'N':  ");
    scanf("%1s", &TestChar);
    if (tolower(TestChar) == 'y') {
    /* First open the printer. If the open fails, stop */
        if (!(ListOut = fopen(PRINTERNAME, "w"))) {
            fprintf(stderr, "Can't get the printer to respond.");
            exit(1);
        }
    /* Print the report multiple times until the user wants to stop. */
        while (tolower(TestChar) == 'y') {
            GenerateReport(ListOut);
    /* Flush the buffer to complete the printout. */
            fflush(ListOut);
    /* Send a formfeed and bell to the printer. */
            fprintf(ListOut, "\f\7");
    /* Query the user. */
            Prompt("\nRepeat the printout? 'Y' or 'N': ");
            scanf("%1s", &TestChar);
        }
    }
}                               /* main */

/* GenerateReport lists the report to the target file */
void GenerateReport(OutFile)
FILE * OutFile;                 /* Target File */
{                               /* GenerateReport */
    int     NumInRpt;           /* Loop variable */

 /* Print banner and basic information. */
    WriteSolidLine(OutFile, 70, 2);
    fprintf(OutFile,
          "\n                   SALES POWER REPORT\n\n");
    WriteSolidLine(OutFile, 70, 2);
    fprintf(OutFile,
         "\n   PERIOD COVERED:  %s to %s\n", StartDate, EndDate);
    fprintf(OutFile,
         "   DATE PREPARED:   %s\n\n", TodaysDate);
    fprintf(OutFile,
         "   TOTAL SALES:  %10.2f\n", TotalSales);
    fprintf(OutFile,
         "   AVERAGE SALES LEVEL:  %10.2f\n\n", AvgSales);
    WriteSolidLine(OutFile, 70, 2);

    fprintf(OutFile,
         "      RECORD #          SALES $       ");
    fprintf(OutFile,
         "$ ABOVE AVGE      $ BELOW AVGE\n");
    WriteSolidLine(OutFile, 70, 2);

 /* Print information on each item. */
    for (NumInRpt = 0; NumInRpt < NumIds; NumInRpt++) {
        fprintf(OutFile, "        %d          %10.2f",
                NumInRpt + 1, SalesAmt[NumInRpt]);
        if (SalesAmt[NumInRpt] > AvgSales)
            fprintf(OutFile, "        %10.2f\n",
```

```
                    SalesAmt[NumInRpt] - AvgSales);
        else
            fprintf(OutFile,
              "                              %10.2f\n",
                    AvgSales - SalesAmt[NumInRpt]);
    }
    WriteSolidLine(OutFile, 70, 2);
}                                   /* GenerateReport */

/* Gets starting information. */
void StartingConditions() {         /* StartingConditions */
    int     IdCntr;                 /* Loop variable */

    printf(
          "What period of time does this report cover?\n");
    printf(
          "(Please enter all dates in the format MM/DD/YY).\n\n")
    Prompt(
          "Start date:   ");
    fgets(StartDate, MAXSTRLEN, stdin);
    StripReturns(StartDate);
    Prompt(
          "End date:     ");
    fgets(EndDate, MAXSTRLEN, stdin);
    StripReturns(EndDate);
    Prompt(
          "Today's date: ");
    fgets(TodaysDate, MAXSTRLEN, stdin);
    StripReturns(TodaysDate);
    printf(
          "\nWHEN PROMPTED, ENTER THE SALES AMOUNT ");
    printf(
          "FOR EACH RECORD.\n");
    printf(
          "TO END THE PROGRAM, TYPE -1 WHEN ASKED FOR AN ENTRY.\n\n");

 /* Continue looping and retrieving information until the user
    enters a -1. */
    do {
        printf("$ Amount for Record Number %d: ", NumIds + 1);
        fflush(stdout);
        scanf("%f", &SalesAmt[NumIds]);
        if (SalesAmt[NumIds] > -1) {
            TotalSales += SalesAmt[NumIds];
            NumIds++;
        }
    } while (SalesAmt[NumIds] != -1 && NumIds != MAXNUMIDS);
    AvgSales = TotalSales / (float) NumIds;
    printf("\n\n\n");
}                                   /* StartingConditions */
```

from this report to maintain the confidentiality of the information.

Let's follow the interaction as the user at the keyboard responds to the screen's queries about each item or person. Our trial responses to the questions are shown in bold:

```
***********************************
SALESPWR — Sales Power Report
***********************************
What Period Of Time Does This Report Cover?
(Please Enter All Dates In The Format MM/DD/YY).
Start Date:              04/01/86
End Date:                04/30/86
Today's Date:            05/07/86


WHEN PROMPTED, ENTER THE SALES AMOUNT FOR EACH RECORD.
TO END THE PROGRAM, TYPE -1 WHEN ASKED FOR AN ENTRY.
```

```
*******************************************************************

                    SALES POWER REPORT

*******************************************************************

PERIOD COVERED:  04/01/86 to 04/30/86
DATE PREPARED:   05/07/86

TOTAL SALES:  1617967.50
AVERAGE SALES LEVEL:   161796.75

*******************************************************************
   RECORD #          SALES $       $ ABOVE AVGE      $ BELOW AVGE
*******************************************************************
       1            123456.78                          38339.97
       2            154321.66                           7475.09
       3            193456.44        31659.69
       4            203456.88        41660.13
       5            174532.33        12735.58
       6            123456.78                          38339.97
       7            165432.13         3635.38
       8            135416.88                          26379.88
       9            144456.42                          17340.33
      10            199981.22        38184.47
*******************************************************************
```

Fig. 19-2. Report produced by SALESPWR.

$ Amount for Record 1:	**123456.78**
$ Amount for Record 2:	**154321.65**
$ Amount for Record 3:	**193456.43**
$ Amount for Record 4:	**203456.87**
$ Amount for Record 5:	**174532.33**
$ Amount for Record 6:	**123456.78**
$ Amount for Record 7:	**165432.12**
$ Amount for Record 8:	**135416.88**
$ Amount for Record 9:	**144456.42**
$ Amount for Record 10:	**199981.22**
$ Amount for Record 11:	**−1**

When we type −1 and press Enter in response to the request for information concerning record 11, the screen clears and the full report is displayed.

If we respond Y to the option to make a printout, a printed copy is produced as shown in Fig. 19-2.

20

TDVAR: Time and Dollar Variance Program

Things often do not go exactly as planned in the business world. If the plan calls for the start of a project on a specific day and the project actually starts on a different day, there is a variance between the actual and start dates. The same holds true for the completion day. Also, plans call for the expenditure of specific dollar amounts on a project or against a chart of accounts. If the actual expenditure is different from the planned amount there is a variance.

Usual practice is to express a variance as a percentage of the planned time or dollars. Also, the variance may be expressed in units, such as "time" or "dollars." The quantified differences between actual and planned performances are the *variances*. Profits, as well as costs, may be considered in terms of variance.

For example, if we are considering time-variances in evaluating the start day for a project and the project starts one or more days later than planned, there is a negative variance. If the start is earlier, it may be considered a positive variance.

When considering dollar expenditures or costs we have a different philosophy. If the actual dollars are less than the planned dollars, we have a positive variance in percent and in pure dollars.

We'll use time variance to demonstrate the capabilities of the program, TDVAR (Fig. 20-1), which takes data supplied through the keyboard and does the comparisons and calculations between actual and planned results. the conclusions are sent to the printer, which prepares a complete, formatted report.

Fig. 20-1. Source code for TDVAR.

```
/* TDVAR -- Copyright 1986 -- T. O. Sidebottom/L. A. Wortman  */

/*      Include Files
*/
#include <stdio.h>
#include <ctype.h>

/*      Definitions
*/
#define FALSE   0
#define MAXSTRLEN 255
#define PRINTERNAME "prn"
#define TRUE    1

/*      External declarations
*/
#include "utildefn.h"

/* Forward declarations
*/
void DollarReport();
void TimeReport();

/*      Global variables
*/
FILE * ListOut;                     /* File opened to printer */

/* Main program
*/
main() {                            /* main */
    char    Check;                  /* Temporary variable */
    char    Dummy[MAXSTRLEN];       /* Temporary variable */
    char    Response[2];            /* Receives user input */

 /* Print startup banner, and open the printer. */
    SignOn("VARIANCES -- Plans Versus Actuals", 19, 70, 0);

    printf("\n\n\n\n\n");
    printf("\t\t\t*** TURN ON THE PRINTER ***\n\n\n\n\n\n");
    WaitFiveSeconds();
    if (!(ListOut = fopen(PRINTERNAME, "w"))) {
        fprintf("Can't seem to get to the printer for output.");
        exit(1);
    }

 /* Let user choose which report to do. */
    Prompt("T)ime or D)ollar variance: ");
    scanf("%1s", Response);
    Check = tolower(Response[0]);
    while (Check != 't' && Check != 'd') {
        Prompt("Please enter 'T' for Time, or 'D' for Dollar: ");
        scanf("%1s", Response);
```

```
        Check = tolower(Response[0]);
    }

 /* Prepare for reporting by clearing the screen and disposing of extra
    characters left behind by scanf. */
    ClearScreen();
    fgets(Dummy, MAXSTRLEN, stdin);

 /* Do report. */
    if (Check == 't')
        TimeReport();
    else
        DollarReport();
}                               /* main */

/* Does dollar variance report.
*/
void DollarReport() {           /* DollarReport */
    float   ActualDollars;      /* Actual dollars */
    int     Counter;            /* Loop variable */
    char    Date[MAXSTRLEN];
    float   DollarVariance;     /* Actual dollar variance */
    char    Dummy[MAXSTRLEN];   /* Temporary */
    int     NumTasks;           /* Number of tasks */
    float   PlanDollars;        /* Planned dollars */
    char    TaskName[MAXSTRLEN];/* Task name */
    char    Title[MAXSTRLEN];   /* Report title */
    float   Variance;           /* Planned versus actual variance */

/* Print banner and collect basic information. */
   printf("\t\tDOLLAR VARIANCE REPORT\n\n");

   Prompt("Enter the date:  ");
   fgets(Date, MAXSTRLEN, stdin);
   StripReturns(Date);
   Prompt("Enter the title: ");
   fgets(Title, MAXSTRLEN, stdin);
   StripReturns(Title);

/* Print banner to printer. */
   WriteSolidLine(ListOut, 72, 0);
   fprintf(ListOut, "                         ");
   fprintf(ListOut, "DOLLAR VARIANCE REPORT\n");
   WriteSolidLine(ListOut, 72, 0);
   fprintf(ListOut, "Date: %10s        Title: %s\n", Date, Title);
   WriteSolidLine(ListOut, 72, 0);
   fprintf(ListOut, "Task Name:                           $-Plan");
   fprintf(ListOut, "        $-Actl       $-Var       %%-Var\n");
   WriteSolidLine(ListOut, 72, 0);
   fprintf(ListOut, "\n");

/* Collect data on all tasks. */
   Prompt("\nHow many tasks to report? ");
   scanf("%d", &NumTasks);
   for (Counter = 0; Counter < NumTasks; Counter++) {
```

```
    /* For each task, get its name and list it to the printer. */
        fgets(Dummy, MAXSTRLEN, stdin);
        printf("\nEnter name of task %d: ", Counter + 1);
        fflush(stdout);
        fgets(TaskName, MAXSTRLEN, stdin);
        StripReturns(TaskName);
        fprintf(ListOut, "%d: %-15s", Counter + 1, TaskName);

    /* Get the financial data. */
        Prompt("Enter planned dollars: ");
        scanf("%f", &PlanDollars);
        fprintf(ListOut, "          %10.2f", PlanDollars);
        Prompt("Enter actual dollars:  ");
        scanf("%f", &ActualDollars);
        fprintf(ListOut, "  %10.2f", ActualDollars);
     /* Print the results. */
         Variance = PlanDollars - ActualDollars;
         printf("Dollar variance is: %10.2f\n", Variance);
         fprintf(ListOut, " %10.2f", Variance);
         printf("Percentage variance is: %9.2f%%\n",
                Variance / PlanDollars * 100.0);
         fprintf(ListOut, " %9.2f%%\n",
                Variance / PlanDollars * 100.0);
    }

    fprintf(ListOut, "\n");
    WriteSolidLine(ListOut, 72, 0);
}                               /* DollarReport */

/* Perform time variance report
*/
void TimeReport() {             /* TimeReport */
    float   ActualStart;        /* Actual start time */
    float   ActualCompleted;    /* Actual completion time */
    int     Counter;            /* Loop variable */
    char    Date[MAXSTRLEN];    /* Today's date */
    char    Dummy[MAXSTRLEN];   /* Temporary */
    int     NumTasks;           /* Number of tasks to analyze */
    float   Planned;            /* Planned starting and ending time */
    char    TaskName[MAXSTRLEN];
    char    Title[MAXSTRLEN];   /* Report title */
    float   Variance;           /* Planned versus actual variance */

  /* Print a starting banner, and collect basic information. */
    printf("\t\tTIME VARIANCE REPORT\n\n");

    Prompt("Enter the date:  ");
    fgets(Date, MAXSTRLEN, stdin);
    StripReturns(Date);
    Prompt("Enter the title: ");
    fgets(Title, MAXSTRLEN, stdin);
    StripReturns(Title);

  /* Print the starting banner to the printer. */
    WriteSolidLine(ListOut, 72, 0);
```

```
    fprintf(ListOut, "                              ");
    fprintf(ListOut, "TIME VARIANCE REPORT\n");
    WriteSolidLine(ListOut, 72, 0);
    fprintf(ListOut, "Date: %10s       Title: %s\n", Date, Title);
    WriteSolidLine(ListOut, 72, 0);
    fprintf(ListOut, "                          -----Start (Day)------  ");
    fprintf(ListOut, "-----Finish (Day)-----  Tot\n");
    fprintf(ListOut, "Task name:           Plan  Actl  Var  %%-Var  ");
    fprintf(ListOut, "Plan  Actl  Var  %%-Var  Days\n");
    WriteSolidLine(ListOut, 72, 0);
    fprintf(ListOut, "\n");

/* Collect data on each task. */
    Prompt("\nHow many tasks to report? ");
    scanf("%d", &NumTasks);
    for (Counter = 0; Counter < NumTasks; Counter++) {

    /* For each task, get its name and print it. */
        fgets(Dummy, MAXSTRLEN, stdin);
        printf("\nEnter name of task %d: ", Counter + 1);
        fflush(stdout);
        fgets(TaskName, MAXSTRLEN, stdin);
        StripReturns(TaskName);
        fprintf(ListOut, "%2d: %-15s", Counter + 1, TaskName);

    /* Get time information. */
        Prompt("Enter planned starting day: ");
        scanf("%f", &Planned);
        fprintf(ListOut, "  %2.0f", Planned);
        Prompt("Enter actual starting day: ");
        scanf("%f", &ActualStart);
        fprintf(ListOut, "   %2.0f", ActualStart);
        Variance = Planned - ActualStart;

    /* Compute and report variance information. */
        printf("Time variance in days is: %2.0f\n", Variance);
        fprintf(ListOut, "    %2.0f", Variance);
        printf("Percentage variance is: %5.1f\n",
                Variance / Planned * 100.0);
        fprintf(ListOut, "  %5.1f", Variance / Planned * 100.0);
        printf("\n");

    /* Get completion day information. */
        Prompt("Enter planned completion day: ");
        scanf("%f", &Planned);
        fprintf(ListOut, "    %2.0f", Planned);
        Prompt("Enter actual completion day:  ");
        scanf("%f", &ActualCompleted);
        fprintf(ListOut, "   %2.0f", ActualCompleted);

    /* Compute and report variance information */
        Variance = Planned - ActualCompleted;
        printf("Time variance in days is: %2.0f\n", Variance);
        fprintf(ListOut, "   %2.0f", Variance);
        printf("Percentage variance is: %5.1f\n",
```

```
                Variance / Planned * 100.0);
        fprintf(ListOut, "  %5.1f", Variance / Planned * 100.0);
        printf("Total number of project days is: %2.0f\n",
                ActualCompleted - ActualStart);
        fprintf(ListOut, "   %2.0f\n", ActualCompleted - ActualStart);
        printf("\n");
    }

    fprintf(ListOut, "\n");
    WriteSolidLine(ListOut, 72, 0);
}                                   /* TimeReport */
```

The interaction between the operator at the keyboard and the program's display on the screen are self-guiding. In this example run, the keyboard responses are shown in bold.

First, the program signs on with a banner:

```
*****************************************
    VARIANCES — Plans versus Actuals
*****************************************
```

Then the screen clears and this message is displayed for a few seconds:

*** TURN ON THE PRINTER ***

Again the screen clears and we are offered a choice:

T)ime or D)ollar Variance: **T**

By entering the letter T at the keyboard we have selected the time variance function. The screen clears and the collection of data begins. Requests for information to be entered appear on the screen, as shown below. The users responses are shown in bold characters beside the queries:

TIME VARIANCE REPORT

Enter the date: **10/31/86**
Enter the title: **Johnstone Proj**

At this point the printer goes into action and prints the headings for the report. The action at the screen continues:

How many tasks to report? **3**
Enter name of task 1: **BlueBird Condo**
Enter planned starting day:$ **23**
Enter actual starting day:$ **26**

Note: instead of dealing with the day, month and year, the start and completion days are counted from the beginning of the calendar or fiscal year, which is day one. The program rapidly calculates the variances and displays them on the screen:

> Time variance in days is: −3
> Percentage variance is: −13.0
>
> Enter planned completion day: **295**
> Enter actual completion day: **290**
> Time variance in days is: 5
> Percentage variance is: 1.7
> Total number of project days is: 264

The program continues with the next request:

> Enter name of task 2: **GreenBird**
> Enter planned starting day: **29**
> Enter actual starting day: **27**
> Time variance in days is: 2
> Percentage variance is: 6.9
>
> Entcr plannod complotion day: **255**
> Enter actual completion day: **257**
> Time variance in days is: −12
> Percentage variance is: −0.8
> Total number of project days is: 230
>
> Enter name of task 3: **YellowBird**
> Enter planned starting day: **44**
> Enter actual starting day: **51**

```
*************************************************************************
                        TIME VARIANCE REPORT
*************************************************************************
Date:    10/31/86          Title: Johnstone Proj
*************************************************************************
                     -----Start (Day)------  -----Finish (Day)-----  Tot
Task name:           Plan  Actl  Var  %-Var  Plan  Actl  Var  %-Var  Days
*************************************************************************

 1: BlueBird Condo   23    26    -3   -13.0  295   290    5    1.7   264
 2: GreenBird        29    27     2     6.9  255   257   -2   -0.8   230
 3: YellowBird       44    51    -7   -15.9  312   312    0    0.0   261

*************************************************************************
```

Fig. 20-2. Time variance report.

```
***************************************************************************
                        DOLLAR VARIANCE REPORT
***************************************************************************
Date:    10/31/86        Title: Johnstone Proj
***************************************************************************
Task Name:                     $-Plan       $-Actl        $-Var        %-Var
***************************************************************************


1: BlueBird Condo            135678.91    129888.99      5789.91        4.27%
2: GreenBird                 159456.23    160333.77      -877.53       -0.55%
3: YellowBird                234567.00    234567.00         0.00        0.00%

***************************************************************************
```

Fig. 20-3. Dollar variance report.

Time variance in days is: −7
Percentage variance is: −15.9

Enter planned completion day: **312**
Enter actual completion day: **312**
Time variance in days is: 0
Percentage variance is: 0.0
Total number of project days is: 261

The system prompt appears at the screen. The buffer dumps the complete report to the printer, as shown in Fig. 20-2, a report actually generated by the sample run.

Choosing the dollar variance function to track variances in costs for the same three projects generates Fig. 20-3.

21

TRAVEXP: Travel Expense Calculator and Report Writer

You are not expected to make a profit on the expense money you spend on business travel. Neither are you expected to take a loss on money spent out-of-pocket on behalf of your company. A detailed set of data with carefully prepared arithmetic for subtotals and totals of the various categories of expenses, together with supporting vouchers or receipts, are essential to the expense recovery or reimbursement to you by the company. Further, the IRS requires a detailed a log of all business-related travel expenses and is reputed to react more favorably to a set of records that are well organized, well maintained and substantiated, than to a messy collection of papers and scratchpad notes.

TRAVEXP, Fig. 21-1, provides a printed report of accurately calculated data for the use of your personal or rental-automobile, and for non-automobile expenses incurred during a business trip. The report fills a single 8.5 × 11-inch sheet of paper that can be bound into a personal record book, and the report can be attached to your company's formal business expense report form.

Want to have a record of what the travel expenses were on your vacation? TRAVEXP also can be used to keep track of the various expense categories that involve non-business travel.

As the diverse categories of information appear on the screen, a built-in time-delay function holds the screen's display so you can read it. Then the information automatically scrolls up and off the screen to display another set of information.

Let's take a trial run.After the program displays its name banner, a set of instructions appears on the screen:

Fig. 21-1. Source code for TRAVEXP.

```
/* TRAVEXP - COPYRIGHT 1986 by T. O. Sidebottom/L. A. Wortman */

/*      Include Files
*/
#include <stdio.h>
#include <ctype.h>

/*      Definitions
*/
#define FALSE   0
#define MAXSTRLEN 255
#define PRINTERNAME "prn"
#define TRUE    1

/*      Code macros
*/
#define IsAutoUsed      ((tolower(UseAuto) == 'y') ? TRUE : FALSE)

/*      External declarations
*/
#include "utildefn.h"

/*      Forward declarations
*/
void AutoOut();
void BasicOut();
void Describe();
void GetAutoData();
void GetBasicData();
void GetMiscData();
float GetValue();
void MiscOut();

/*      Global variables
*/
float   Airplane;               /* Airplane costs */
float   AutoCosts = 0.0;        /* Automobile costs */
float   CarMaintain;            /* Car maintenance costs */
float   CarRent;                /* Car rental costs */
char    Cities[MAXSTRLEN];      /* List of cities visited */
char    Days[MAXSTRLEN];        /* List of days */
char    DateEnd[MAXSTRLEN];     /* Ending day */
char    DateStart[MAXSTRLEN];   /* Starting day */

float   DrivTime;               /* Driving time */
float   Entertain;              /* Entertainment costs */
float   Fuel;                   /* Fuel amount */
float   FuelPrice;              /* Fuel price */
int     I;                      /* Loop variable */
float   Laundry;                /* Laundry costs */
FILE * ListOut;                 /* File opened to printer */
float   Lodging;                /* Lodging costs */
float   Meals;                  /* Cost of meals */
```

```
float   Miles;                   /* Number of miles traveled */
float   Misc;                    /* Miscellaneous  */
float   MiscCosts = 0.0;
float   Oil;                     /* Oil use */
float   Parking;                 /* Parking fees */
float   Phone;                   /* Phone costs */
float   Taxis;                   /* Taxi costs */
float   Tips;                    /* Cost of tips */
float   Tolls;                   /* Cost of tolls */
float   Trains;                  /* Cost of trains */
char    TripPurpose[MAXSTRLEN];  /* Description of trip's purpose */
char    UseAuto;                 /* Flag indicating if car was used. */

/*      Main program
*/
main(argc, argv)
int     argc;
char   *argv[];
{                                /* main */
    int     Counter;             /* Loop variable */

 /* List the starting banner, followed by an explanation
    of how to use this program. */
    SignOn("TRAVEXP -- Record of Travel Expenses", 10, 66, 0);
    ClearScreen();
    Describe();
    WaitFiveSeconds() + WaitFiveSeconds();

 /* Get starting information. */
    ClearScreen();
    GetBasicData();

 /* If a car was used on this trip, get additional information. */
    if (IsAutoUsed)
        GetAutoData();
    GetMiscData();
    WaitFiveSeconds();
 /* Write the report to the screen. */
    ClearScreen();
    BasicOut(stdout);
    if (IsAutoUsed)
        AutoOut(stdout);
    WaitFiveSeconds();
    MiscOut(stdout);

 /* Send the report to the printer. */
    printf("\nTurn On The Printer. Check And Adjust The Paper.\n\n");
    WaitFiveSeconds();
    WaitFiveSeconds();
 /* Open the printer. If the open fails, stop. */
    if (!(ListOut = fopen(PRINTERNAME, "w"))) {
        fprintf(stderr, "Can't open printer.");
        exit(1);
    }
    ClearScreen();
```

```
    printf("\t\t*** Hard-Copy Is Now Being Printed ***\n\n\n\n\n\n");
    BasicOut(ListOut);
    if (IsAutoUsed)
        AutoOut(ListOut);
    MiscOut(ListOut);

    fprintf(ListOut, "\nTOTAL TRAVEL EXPENSES: $%10.2f\n\n",
            AutoCosts + MiscCosts);
    WriteSolidLine(ListOut, 60, 0);
}                               /* main */

/* AutoOut writes information about car expenses
   to the target file. */
void AutoOut(OutFile)
FILE * OutFile;                 /* Target file */
{                               /* AutoOut */
    fprintf(OutFile,
            "\nThe Following Are Autombile Operating Expenses:\n\n");
    fprintf(OutFile,
            "Travel included %6.2f miles of driving.\n", Miles);
    fprintf(OutFile,
            "The automobile got %5.2f miles per gallon or litre.\n",
            Miles / Fuel);
    fprintf(OutFile, "Speed averaged %5.2f miles per hour.\n",
            Miles / DrivTime);
    fprintf(OutFile, "Fuel cost was $%5.2f per mile.\n",
            FuelPrice / (Miles / Fuel));

    fprintf(OutFile, "Total fuel cost for the trip: $%5.2f\n",
            FuelPrice * Fuel);
    fprintf(OutFile, "Tolls paid: $%5.2f\n", Tolls);
    fprintf(OutFile, "Parking fees: $%5.2f\n", Parking);
    fprintf(OutFile, "Oil added at a cost of: $%5.2f\n", Oil);
    fprintf(OutFile, "Repairs/Maintenance costs: $%5.2f\n",
            CarMaintain);
    AutoCosts = FuelPrice * Fuel + Oil + CarMaintain + Tolls +
        Parking;
    fprintf(OutFile, "Cost of operation per mile: $%5.2f\n",
            AutoCosts / Miles);
    fprintf(OutFile,
            "\nTOTAL COST FOR %5.2f MILES OF AUTOMOBILE OPERATION: $%5.2f\n\n",
            Miles, AutoCosts);
}                               /* AutoOut */

/* Prints fundamental information about the analysis. */
void BasicOut(OutFile) {        /* BasicOut */
    WriteSolidLine(OutFile, 60, 0);
    fprintf(OutFile, "\nTRAVEL EXPENSE REPORT: %s through %s",
            DateStart, DateEnd);
    fprintf(OutFile, "\nPurpose Of The %s Day Trip Was: %s ",
            Days, TripPurpose);
    fprintf(OutFile, "\nCities Visited Were: \n");
    fprintf(OutFile, " %s\n\n",
            Cities);
    WriteSolidLine(OutFile, 60, 0);
}                               /* BasicOut */
```

```
/* Describes how to use this program. */
void Describe() {                   /* Describe */
    printf("THE FOLLOWING INSTRUCTIONS WILL BE ");
    printf("DISPLAYED FOR 10 SECONDS:\n\n\n");
    printf("This program provides information\n");
    printf("concerning all travel expenses,\n");
    printf("including the costs of using an\n");
    printf("automobile...company or personal.\n\n");
    printf("Answer the questions and enter amounts.\n");
    printf("The computer will do all calculations.\n\n");
    printf("If an amount is zero, enter a zero (0).\n");
    printf("Press the ENTER key, and continue.\n\n");
    printf("A hard-copy report is generated automatically.\n\n");
    printf("(Be Sure Your Printer Is Turned On!)\n");
}                                   /* Describe */
/* Retrieves information about automobile use. */
void GetAutoData() {                /* GetAutoData */
    Miles = GetValue("How many miles did you drive? ");
    Fuel = GetValue(
            "How many gallons or litres of gas did you use? ");
    FuelPrice = GetValue(
            "What price did you pay per gallon or litre? ");
    DrivTime = GetValue(
            "What was the driving time in hours? ");
    printf("\n\nHow Much Did You Spend For: \n\n");
    Tolls = GetValue("Tolls? ");
    Parking = GetValue("Parking? ");
    Oil = GetValue("Oil? ");
    CarMaintain = GetValue("Car repairs or maintenance? ");
}                                   /* GetAutoData */

/* Retrieves fundamental information about the trip. */
void GetBasicData() {               /* GetBasicData */
    char    Response[2];            /* Receives character input from user */

 /* Prompt and read character information describing the trip. */
    Prompt("What Was The Trip's Purpose? (Use Only One line): ");
    fgets(TripPurpose, MAXSTRLEN, stdin);
    StripReturns(TripPurpose);
    Prompt("\nHow Many Days Did The Trip Take? ");
    fgets(Days, MAXSTRLEN, stdin);
    StripReturns(Days);
    Prompt("What Was The Starting Date? (MM/DD/YY): ");
    fgets(DateStart, MAXSTRLEN, stdin);
    StripReturns(DateStart);
    Prompt("What Was The Ending Date? (MM/DD/YY):   ");
    fgets(DateEnd, MAXSTRLEN, stdin);
    StripReturns(DateEnd);
    printf("\n\nWhat Cities Did You Visit?\n");
    printf(" (Put Spaces -- Not Punctuations -- Between City Names.\n");
    printf(" All Entries On One Line Only. Abbreviate If Necessary.):\n ");
    fgets(Cities, MAXSTRLEN, stdin);
    StripReturns(Cities);
    printf("\n");
```

```
/* Determine if a car was used. If so, set UseAuto to 'y'. */
   do {
       Prompt("Did You Use Your Own Automobile On This Trip? (Y/N): ");
       scanf("%1s", Response);
       UseAuto = tolower(Response[0]);
   } while (UseAuto != 'y' && UseAuto != 'n');

       printf("\nYou %s use your own automobile on this trip.\n\n",
               (UseAuto == 'y') ? "DID" : "DID NOT");
   }                                /* GetBasicData */

   /* Retrieve non-automobile expense information. */
   void GetMiscData() {             /* GetMiscData */
       printf("\n\n");
       printf("List The Amounts Paid For Non-Automobile Expenses: \n\n");
       Airplane = GetValue("Airplanes: ");
       Trains = GetValue("Trains: ");
       Taxis = GetValue("Taxicabs: ");
       CarRent = GetValue("Car rental (if applicable): ");
       Meals = GetValue("Meals: ");
       Lodging = GetValue("Lodging: ");
       Phone = GetValue("Telephone: ");
       Tips = GetValue("Tips: ");
       Entertain = GetValue("Business entertainment: ");
       Laundry = GetValue("Laundry and tailor services: ");
       Misc = GetValue("Miscellaneous: ");
   }                                /* GetMiscData */

   /* Write a prompt and return the floating point value entered. */
   float   GetValue(DisplayString)
   char   *DisplayString;           /* Prompt to write */
   {                                /* GetValue */
       float   Temp;                /* Floating point number read */

       Prompt(DisplayString);
       scanf("%f", &Temp);
       return(Temp);
   }                                /* GetValue */

   /* Write non-automobile miscellaneous report information
      to the output file. */
   void MiscOut(OutFile)
   FILE * OutFile;                  /* Target file */
   {                                /* MiscOut */
       fprintf(OutFile, "\nThe Following Are Non-Automobile Expenses: \n\n");
       fprintf(OutFile, "Airplane fares: $%7.2f\n", Airplane);
       fprintf(OutFile, "Train fares: $%6.2f\n", Trains);
       fprintf(OutFile, "Taxicab fares: $%6.2f\n", Taxis);
       fprintf(OutFile, "Car rentals: $%6.2f\n", CarRent);
       fprintf(OutFile, "Meals purchased for self: $%6.2f\n",
               Meals);
       fprintf(OutFile, "Lodgings: $%6.2f\n", Lodging);
       fprintf(OutFile, "Telephone calls: $%6.2f\n", Phone);
       fprintf(OutFile, "Tips paid: $%6.2f\n", Tips);
       fprintf(OutFile, "Business entertainment: $%6.2f\n",
```

```
            Entertain);
    fprintf(OutFile, "Laundry and tailor services: $%6.2f\n",
            Laundry);
    fprintf(OutFile,
            "Miscellaneous (not covered elsewhere): $%6.2f\n",
            Misc);
    MiscCosts = Meals + Misc + Airplane + Trains + Taxis +
        Phone + Tips + Lodging + Entertain + CarRent + Laundry;
    fprintf(OutFile,
            "\nTOTAL EXPENSES, EXCLUDING AUTOMOBILE OPERATION: $%8.2f\n\n",
            MiscCosts);
    WriteSolidLine(OutFile, 60, 0);
}                                   /* MiscOut */
```

This program provides information
concerning all travel expenses,
including the cost of using an
automobile. . .company or personal.

Answer the questions and the
computer will do the calculations.

If a question isn't applicable,
enter a zero, 0.

Press the Enter key, and continue.

A hard copy report is automatic.
(Be Sure Your Printer Is Turned On!)

After a ten-second delay for reading, the series of questions dealing with the specific trip starts. Responses to the questions in this sample run are shown in bold:

What Was The Trip's Purpose? (Use Only One Line):
Sales Calls
How Many Days Did The Trip Take? **5**
What Was The Starting Date? (MM/DD/YY): **10/02/86**
What Was The Ending Date? (MM/DD/YY): **10/06/86**
What Cities Did You Visit?
(Put Spaces — Not Punctuations — Between City Names.
All Entries On One Line Only. Abbreviate If Necessary.):
Detroit Chicago Dallas Austin Houston
Did You Use Your Own Automobile On This Trip? (Y/N): **Y**

If you had keyed the letter N the program would have confirmed your response by displaying:

You DID NOT use your own automobile on this trip.

Also, the program would have skipped the next portion of the questions and moved directly to the non-automobile expense section (which comes up later). However, because you responded with Y, the program continues:

```
You DID use your own automobile on this trip.
How many miles did you drive?  1254
How many gallons or liters of gas did you use?  83.6
What price did you pay per gallon or liter?  1.47
What was the driving time in hours?  25.5

How Much Did You Spend For:
Tolls?  12.5
Parking?  23.75
Oil?  0
Car repairs or maintenance?  29.95

List The Amounts Paid For Non-Automobile Expenses:
Airplanes:  123.56
Trains:  0
Taxicabs:  23.57
Car rental (if applicable):  0
Meals:  232.55
Lodging:  487.9
Telephone:  87.63
Tips:  25
Business entertainment:  134.66
Laundry and tailor services:  5.85
Miscellaneous:  0
```

After the last entry is made (Miscellaneous:) and you press the enter key, the screen clears and displays a comprehensive analysis of the automobile expenses:

```
************************************************************
TRAVEL EXPENSE REPORT:     10/02/86 through 10/06/86
Purpose Of The 5 Day Trip Was:     Sales Calls
Cities Visited Were:
Detroit  Chicago  Dallas  Austin  Houston
************************************************************
The Following Are Automobile Operating Expenses:
Travel included 1254.00 miles of driving.
The automobile got 15.00 miles per gallon or liter.
Speed averaged 49.18 miles per hour.
Fuel cost was $ 0.10 per mile.
Total fuel cost for the trip:  $122.89
```

Tolls paid: $12.50
Parking fees: $23.75
Oil added at a cost of $ 0.00
Repairs/Maintenance costs: $29.95
Cost of operation per mile: $ 0.15
TOTAL COST FOR 1254.00 MILES OF AUTOMOBILE OPERATION: $189.09

The text scrolls automatically and more details are displayed:

The Following Are Non-Automobile Expenses:
Airplane fares: $123.56
Train fares: $ 0.00
Taxicab fares: $ 23.57
Car rentals: $ 0.00
Meals purchased for self: $232.55
Lodgings: $487.90
Telephone calls: $ 87.63
Tips paid: $ 25.00
Business entertainment: $134.66
Laundry and tailor services: $ 5.85
Miscellaneous (not covered elsewhere): $ 0.00
TOTAL EXPENSES, EXCLUDING AUTOMOBILE OPERATIONS: $ 1120.72

At this point in the program's progress, the bottom of the screen displays the notice:

Turn On The Printer. Check And Adjust The Paper.

Within a few seconds the expense information that had been displayed on the screen is sent to the printer, which generates this report. Note, too, the final summary line that is automatically added to the bottom of the printed copy (Fig. 21-2).

Fig. 21-2. TRAVEXP report produced by the compiled program.

```
****************************************************************

TRAVEL EXPENSE REPORT: 10/02/86 through 10/06/86
Purpose Of The 5 Day Trip Was: Sales Calls
Cities Visited Were:
 Detroit Chicago Dallas Austin Houston

****************************************************************

The Following Are Autombile Operating Expenses:

Travel included 1254.00 miles of driving.
The automobile got 15.00 miles per gallon or litre.
Speed averaged 49.18 miles per hour.
Fuel cost was $ 0.10 per mile.
Total fuel cost for the trip: $122.89
Tolls paid: $12.50
Parking fees: $23.75
Oil added at a cost of: $ 0.00
Repairs/Maintenance costs: $29.95
Cost of operation per mile: $ 0.15

TOTAL COST FOR 1254.00 MILES OF AUTOMOBILE OPERATION: $189.09


The Following Are Non-Automobile Expenses:

Airplane fares: $ 123.56
Train fares: $  0.00
Taxicab fares: $ 23.57
Car rentals: $  0.00
Meals purchased for self: $232.55
Lodgings: $487.90
Telephone calls: $ 87.63
Tips paid: $ 25.00
Business entertainment: $134.66
Laundry and tailor services: $  5.85
Miscellaneous (not covered elsewhere): $  0.00

TOTAL EXPENSES, EXCLUDING AUTOMOBILE OPERATION: $ 1120.72

****************************************************************

TOTAL TRAVEL EXPENSES: $   1309.81

****************************************************************
```

22

TREND: Trend Analysis Program

Statistics related to a period of time, such as market history, can be difficult to interpret. This is especially true when the data has many peaks and valleys, high and low points. These radical excursions from a smooth line of activity can mask the trend, make it next to impossible to determine whether or not the business, markets, or sales are growing or declining, advancing or retreating.

When supplied with a series of data based on past performance (in units or dollars; no matter), TREND, Fig. 22-1, applies a moving average effect to the data. This tends to smooth the peaks and valleys of the raw data and provide an easier-to-interpret set of data that can shed significant light on the picture. This is best demonstrated with a typical run of the program. (The data produced by TREND can be converted to a graphics display with the PLOTTER program in Chapter 16.)

Let's assume we are dealing with sales dollars over a 15 month period. We could work with a shorter period of time, but the longer period will provide a better analysis. TREND is set to handle up to 50 time periods, which can be seconds, minutes, hours, days, weeks, months, quarters, years, etc.

Calling TREND to the screen causes the sign-on banner to be displayed. The screen clears automatically and displays the first request. All our responses to requests seen on the screen are shown in bold:

```
How Many Time Periods Are To Be Entered? (50 Max):  15
Enter a Value for Each of the 15 Time Periods:
```

Fig. 22-1. Source code for TREND.

```
/* TREND - COPYRIGHT 1986 by T. O. Sidebottom/L. A. Wortman */

/*      Include Files
*/
#include <stdio.h>

/*      Definitions
*/
#define MAXNUMPERIODS 50
#define PRINTERNAME "prn"

/*      External declarations
*/
#include "utildefn.h"

/* Forward declarations
*/
void GenerateReport();
void GetNumToAverage();
void StartingConditions();
void WriteBrokenLine() ;

/*      Global variables
*/
FILE * ListOut;                  /* File opened to printer */
int     NumAveraged;             /* Number of items averaged */
int     NumPeriods;              /* Number of periods to analyse */
float   PeriodValue[MAXNUMPERIODS];/* Values to analyse */
float   TrendValue;              /* Trend of analysis */

/*      Main program
*/
main(argc, argv)
int     argc;
char   *argv[];
{                                /* main */
    char    Response[2];         /* Response from user */
    char    TestChar[2];         /* Temporary character input */
/* Open printer. If open fails, stop, and return to DOS. */
   if (!(ListOut = fopen(PRINTERNAME, "w"))) {
       fprintf(stderr, "Can't open printer.");
       exit(1);
   }

/* Print starting banner. Describe how to use program and collect input
   data. */
   SignOn("TREND - Time Series Analysis/Forecast", 20, 48, 15);
   StartingConditions();
   WaitASecond();
   WaitASecond();
   ClearScreen();
```

```
 /* List report to the display. Repeat, if the user wishes. */
    do {
        GenerateReport(stdout);
        fflush(stdout);
        Prompt("\nRepeat the display? (Y/N): ");
        scanf("%1s", Response);

        if (tolower(Response[0]) == 'y') {
        /* Allow the user to change the number of periods to average. */
            Prompt("Change the number of periods to be averaged? (Y/N): ");
            scanf("%1s", TestChar);
            if (tolower(TestChar[0]) == 'y')
                GetNumToAverage();
        }
    } while (tolower(Response[0]) == 'y');

 /* Print the results. */
    Prompt("\n\nPrintout? Turn on the printer. Type 'Y' or 'N': ");
    scanf("%1s", Response);
    while (tolower(Response[0]) == 'y') {
        GenerateReport(ListOut);
        Prompt("\n\nPrintout? Turn on the printer. Type 'Y' or 'N': ");
        scanf("%1s", Response);
    }
}                               /* main */

/* Print the final results to the target file. */
void GenerateReport(OutFile)
FILE * OutFile;                 /* Target file */
{                               /* GenerateReport */
    int     Counter;            /* Loop variable */
    int     NumSequence;        /* Loop variable */

/* Print the starting report banner. */
   WriteSolidLine(OutFile, 70, 2);
   fprintf(OutFile,
           "\n                  TIME-SERIES TREND ANALYSIS\n\n");
   WriteSolidLine(OutFile, 70, 2);
   fprintf(OutFile, "\n           ");
   fprintf(OutFile, "PERIOD           RAW DATA          SMOOTHED DATA\n");
   WriteBrokenLine(OutFile);
   fprintf(OutFile, "\n");

/* Loop through all items in the list. */
   for (NumSequence = 0; NumSequence < NumPeriods + 1;
           NumSequence++) {
       TrendValue = 0.0;
       if (NumSequence >= NumAveraged) {
       /* If we can, average NumAveraged items to give us the moving
          average. */
           for (Counter = 1; Counter <= NumAveraged; Counter++)
               TrendValue += PeriodValue[NumSequence - Counter];
           TrendValue /= NumAveraged;
       }
       if (NumSequence < NumPeriods)/* Print the averaged value */
```

```
            fprintf(OutFile,
                    "           %7d           %7.1f            %7.1f\n",
                    NumSequence + 1,
                    PeriodValue[NumSequence], TrendValue);
        else {                    /* At the end of the report, print the
                                     forecast based on the trend analysis.
                                  */
            fprintf(OutFile, "\n");
            WriteBrokenLine(OutFile);
            fprintf(OutFile,
              "           The trend forecasts period %d as:      %7.1f\n",
                    NumSequence + 1, TrendValue);
            WriteBrokenLine(OutFile);
            fprintf(OutFile,"           Number of periods averaged: %d\n",
                    NumAveraged);
        }
    }
    fprintf(OutFile, "\n");
    WriteSolidLine(OutFile, 70, 2);
}                                 /* GenerateReport */

/* Get the number to average together for this output run. */
void GetNumToAverage() {          /* GetNumToAverage */
    printf("\nEnter the number of periods to be averaged: ");
    fflush(stdout);
    scanf("%d", &NumAveraged);
    printf("\n");
}                                 /* GetNumToAverage */

/* Retrieve the starting input data. */
void StartingConditions() {       /* StartingConditions */
    int     PeriodCounter;        /* Loop variable */

 /* Get the analysis parameters. */
    Prompt("How many time periods are to be entered? (50 max):  ");
    scanf("%d", &NumPeriods);
    while (NumPeriods >= MAXNUMPERIODS) {
        printf("\nThe number of periods is too large. Maximum is 50.\n");
        Prompt("How many time periods are to be entered? (50 max):  ");
        scanf("%d", &NumPeriods);
    }
    printf("\nEnter a Value for each of the %d time periods :\n\n",
            NumPeriods);
    for (PeriodCounter = 0; PeriodCounter < NumPeriods;
            PeriodCounter++) {
    /* Get the actual analysis values. Prompt for the value, and read it.
    */
        printf("                                     %3d = ",
                PeriodCounter + 1);
        fflush(stdout);
        scanf("%f", &PeriodValue[PeriodCounter]);
    }

 /* Get the number of items to average together. */
    GetNumToAverage();
```

```
    printf("\n\n");
}                                  /* StartingConditions */

void WriteBrokenLine(OutFile)
FILE * OutFile;
{                                  /* WriteBrokenLine */
    fprintf(OutFile,
            "                    ----------------------------------------------
}                                  /* WriteBrokenLine */
```

1 = 123456
2 = 154321
3 = 164322
4 = 114455
5 = 103217
6 = 181235
7 = 183334
8 = 202456
9 = 223545
10 = 211110
11 = 244455
12 = 190022
13 = 253355
14 = 222222
15 = 250066

After completing the fifteenth entry, a new query appears at the bottom of the screen:

Enter the Number of Periods to Be Averaged: **5**

We enter 5 as a first pass. Later the program will give us the opportunity to test several averaging periods until we find the one that is most helpful to us. (At that point a printed copy of the complete table can be made.)

Repeat the Display? (Y/N):

If we respond Y to this query the following line appears on the screen:

Change the Number of Periods to Be Averaged? (Y/N):

By again typing Y and pressing the Enter key we can test the data with a variety of averaging periods. The table will be recalculated and displayed each time we select a new averaging period. The column of raw data (the 15 lines of numbers we entered at the start) remains unchanged. The smoothed data column changes. Also, the forecast for period 16 changes.

In this case, the smoothed data shows that the company's direction is up-

```
**********************************************************************

                     TIME-SERIES TREND ANALYSIS

**********************************************************************

          PERIOD             RAW DATA            SMOOTHED DATA
         ---------------------------------------------------

             1               123456.0                  0.0
             2               154321.0                  0.0
             3               164322.0                  0.0
             4               114455.0                  0.0
             5               103217.0                  0.0
             6               181235.0             131954.2
             7               183334.0             143510.0
             8               202456.0             149312.6
             9               223545.0             156939.4
            10               211110.0             178757.4
            11               244455.0             200336.0
            12               190022.0             212980.0
            13               253355.0             214317.6
            14               222222.0             224497.4
            15               250066.0             224232.8

         ---------------------------------------------------
         The trend forecasts period 16 as:        232024.0
         ---------------------------------------------------
         Number of periods averaged: 5

**********************************************************************
```

Fig. 22-2. Sample run of time series data.

ward despite the wide swings and perturbations in the raw data. How valid is the forecast for period 16? A meaningful forecast must take into account more than the statistical history of raw data, such as experience and special knowledge of economics and other factors that influence the state of the industry. However, TREND does provide a starting point and, in our example, does show a probable advance over period 15.

If we enter the letter N in response to the query to repeat the display, we are asked:

Printout? Turn On the Printer. Type 'Y' or 'N':

Entering Y causes the complete table of information to be sent to the printer; see the example in Fig. 22-2. We are asked the same question after the printing is finished. This enables us to make as many copies as we need. Typing the letter N terminates the program.

23

TESTMATH: Mathematics Skill Tester

Do you wonder whether your compiler (and your computer) are correctly, accurately, calculating and displaying arithmetic?

TESTMATH, Fig. 23-1, is a short but powerful program that will answer your questions and, probably, eliminate all doubts. TESTMATH actually performs the calculations and displays the results for preselected data. (You can alter the data, or add as many complex calculations as you find essential.)

The expected results, which you will have independently calculated, are also displayed. This makes it practical for you to quickly determine whether or not you can depend on your compiler and your computer to operate with mathematical precision.

Figure 23-2 is an actual printout (Shift-PrtSc) of the display taken from the monitor when TESTMATH is run.

Fig. 23-1. Source code for TESTMATH.

```
/* TESTMATH - COPYRIGHT 1986 by T. O. Sidebottom/L. A. Wortman */

/* We declare a variable type and
   assign a value on the same line.
   The values to the right of the
   equate sign can be changed for
   additional tests.
 */
```

```
int     a = 1234;
int     b = 10;
long    c = 1234;
long    d = 5678;
float   e = 1.234;
float   f = 0.5678;
double  g = 1234567.0;
double  h = 1234.0;

main() {

 /* Display the signon banner. First, clear the screen of
    previous material by using newlines. */
    printf("\n\n\n\n\n");
    printf("|=-=-=-=-=-=-=-=-=-=-=-=-=-=-=-=-=-=-=-=-=|\n");
    printf("|  THIS IS THE TESTMATH PROGRAM            |\n");
    printf("|                                          |\n");
    printf("|  It test the C compiler, linker and      |\n");
    printf("|  the libraries.                          |\n");
    printf("|  The number in parentheses must match    |\n");
    printf("|  the calculated number.  Then the        |\n");
    printf("|  compiler is doing its job correctly.    |\n");
    printf("|=-=-=-=-=-=-=-=-=-=-=-=-=-=-=-=-=-=-=-=-=|\n");
    printf("\n");

    printf("Test for INTEGER math: 1234 * 10 = %d\n", a * b);
    printf("(The calculated number should be:  12340)\n\n");

    printf("Test for LONG math: 1234 * 5678 = %ld\n", c * d);
    printf("(The calculated number should be: 7006652)\n\n");
    printf("Test for FLOAT math: 1.234 + 0.5678 = %g\n", e + f);
    printf("(The calculated number should be:     1.8018)\n\n");

    printf("Test for DOUBLE math: 1234567.0 / 1234.0 = %g\n", g / h);
    printf("(The calculated number should be:            1000.459481)\n\n");

    printf("Do the calculations check OK?\n");
}
```

```
|=-=-=-=-=-=-=-=-=-=-=-=-=-=-=-=-=-=-=-=-=|
|  THIS IS THE TESTMATH PROGRAM            |
|                                          |
|  It test the C compiler, linker and      |
|  the libraries.                          |
|  The number in parentheses must match    |
|  the calculated number.  Then the        |
|  compiler is doing its job correctly.    |
|=-=-=-=-=-=-=-=-=-=-=-=-=-=-=-=-=-=-=-=-=|
```

Fig. 23-2. A reproduction of the screen's display made with Shift-PrtSc.

```
Test for INTEGER math: 1234 * 10 = 12340
(The calculated number should be:  12340)

Test for LONG math: 1234 * 5678 = 7006652
(The calculated number should be: 7006652)

Test for FLOAT math: 1.234 + 0.5678 = 1.8018
(The calculated number should be:     1.8018)

Test for DOUBLE math: 1234567.0 / 1234.0 = 1000.459481
(The calculated number should be:          1000.459481)

Do the calculations check OK?
```

24

PACK and UNPACK: ASCII File Concatenator

Have you ever wanted to send, up-load, or down-load a series of text files that have been saved in ASCII? Have you groaned at the thought of having to watch the computer screen waiting for each file to end so you can enter the name of the next file in your queue and finish the job? We have, and we shared your boredom and impatience.

The next two programs, PACK and UNPACK (Figs. 24-1 and 24-2) are treated as a pair. One is not very useful without the other. They do their jobs speedily and without fuss. Instructions about how to use them are included in the comments for the code.

Fig. 24-1. Source code for PACK.

```
/* PACK - convert a group of separately named ASCII text
     files into one continuous file with a common, new name.

   See the How_To function for usage instruction.

   Use UNPACK to separate the PACKed files.
*/

#include "stdio.h"

FILE *Original_Name, *New_Name;
```

```
    main(argc, argv)
    int     argc;
    char    *argv[];
    {
        int     ch,
                Name_Counter;

     if (argc < 3) {
         How_To();
         exit(0);
     }

     argc--;
     if (Status(argv[1])) {
         How_To();
         exit(1);
     }
     if ((New_Name = fopen(argv[1], "w")) == NULL) {
         How_To();
         exit(1);
     }
    for (Name_Counter = 2; Name_Counter <= argc; Name_Counter++) {
        if ((Original_Name = fopen(argv[Name_Counter], "r")) == NULL) {
            Oops(argv[Name_Counter]);
            exit(2);
        }
        fprintf(New_Name, "*FILE: %s\n", argv[Name_Counter]);
        printf("*FILE: %s\n", argv[Name_Counter]);
        while ((ch = getc(Original_Name)) >= 0)
            putc(ch, New_Name);
        fclose(Original_Name);
    }
}

/* Display the message on how to run the program. */
How_To() {
    printf("\nUsage: pack New_Name Original_Name1 Original_Name2 etc...\n");
}

/* Display a trouble message. */
Oops(s)
char    *s;
{
    printf("\nSorry, but I have trouble reading file: %s\n", s);
}

/* Check the status of the names of files being packed together. */
Status(s)
char    *s;
{
    FILE * f;
    if ((f = fopen(s, "r")) == NULL)
        return 0;
    fclose(f);
    return 1;
 }
```

Fig. 24-2. Source code for UNPACK.

```
/* UNPACK - convert a goup of files that have been joined
   together with the PACK program to their original single
   file state.
*/

#include "stdio.h"

#define  Buffer_Size  512

FILE * Original_Name, *New_Name;

main(argc, argv)
int     argc;
char    *argv[];
{
    int     ch;
    char    filename[61];
    char    buf[Buffer_Size];
    int     File_Was_Opened = 0;

    if (argc < 2) {
        How_To();
        exit(0);
    }

    argc--;
    if ((Original_Name = fopen(argv[1], "r")) == NULL)
        Oops();
    while (fgets(buf, Buffer_Size, Original_Name) != NULL) {
        filename[0] = '\0';
        sscanf(buf, "*FILE: %60s", filename);
        if (filename[0] != '\0') {
            if (File_Was_Opened)
                fclose(New_Name);
           printf("*FILE: %s\n", filename);
           if ((New_Name = fopen(filename, "w")) == NULL)
               Oops_Again();
           File_Was_Opened = 1;
           continue;
        }
        if (!File_Was_Opened)
            More_Oops();
        if (fputs(buf, New_Name) == EOF)
            Oops_Again();
    }
    if (ferror(Original_Name))
        Oops();
    fclose(Original_Name);
}

How_To() {
    printf("\nUsage: unpack New_Name\n");
```

```
}

Oops() {
    printf("\nSorry, but I can't read the input file.\n");
    fclose(Original_Name);
    exit(1);
}

Oops_Again() {
    printf("\nSorry again, but I can't create the output file.\n");
    fclose(New_Name);
    exit(1);
}

More_Oops() {
    printf("\nThe file doesn't seem to have been packed with PACK.\n");
    exit(1);
}
```

25

FAHR2CEL and CEL2FAHR: Temperature Conversion Programs

Another interesting example of performing calculations with the C programming language is given in the program FAHR2CEL, Fig. 25-1. Whether or not you are interested in specifically converting Fahrenheit temperatures to Celsius is not the vital issue. The real issue, and our intent in including FAHR2CEL in our group of teaching/learning programs, is to demonstrate the way to rapidly perform a series of calculations, converting data from one set of standards to another.

You might use the same technique for converting fractions to decimals, for example. Try this program as written, and then revise it and do your own experiments. For additional practice, try Fig. 25-2, which converts Fahrenheit to Celsius.

Fig. 25-1. Source code for FAHR2CEL.

```
/* FAHR2CEL - generate and display a fahrenheit
   to celsius conversion table
*/

main() {
    int     Lower_Limit,
            Upper_Limit;
    float   Fahrenheit,
            Celsius,
```

```
            Step;

    Lower_Limit = 0;              /* Initialize the lower limit */
    Upper_Limit = 300;            /* Ditto for the upper limit  */
    Step = 2.5;                   /* Ditto for the step size */

    printf("\nThe following displays the conversion of\n");
    printf("Fahrenheit to Celsius in steps of %2.2f degrees:\n\n", Step);

/* Initialize the value of Fahrenheit to the value of Lower_Limit. */
    Fahrenheit = Lower_Limit;

/* Create and display the headings for the two columns of data. */
    printf("    FAHRENHEIT  CELSIUS\n");
    printf("    ----------  -------\n");

/* Start a loop that calculates the value of Celsius
   while the value Fahrenheit is less than the value
   of the Upper_Limit. The while loop contains the
   formula for the calculations. */
    while (Fahrenheit <= Upper_Limit) {
        Celsius = (5.0 / 9.0) * (Fahrenheit - 32.0);

/* Display the table of data in floating point format. */
        printf("        %3.2f      %3.3f\n", Fahrenheit, Celsius);
        Fahrenheit = Fahrenheit + Step;
    }                             /* end of the "while" loop. */
}                                 /* end of the main function. */
```

Fig. 25-2. Source code for CEL2FAHR.

```
/* CEL2FAHR - generate and display a
   Celsius to Fahrenheit conversion table

   (Note the differences--as well as the
    similarities--with FAH2CEL)
*/

main() {
    int     Lower_Limit,
            Upper_Limit;
    float   Fahrenheit,
            Celsius,
            Step;

    Lower_Limit = 0;              /* Initialize the lower limit */
    Upper_Limit = 300;            /* Ditto for the upper limit  */
    Step = 2.5;                   /* Ditto for the step size */

    printf("\nThe following displays the conversion of\n");
    printf("Celsius to Fahrenheit in steps of %2.2f degrees:\n\n", Step);
```

```
/* Initialize the value of Celsius to the value of Lower_Limit. */
    Celsius = Lower_Limit;

/* Create and display the headings for the two columns of data. */
    printf("     CELSIUS   FAHRENHEIT\n");
    printf("     -------   ----------\n");

/* Create a loop that calculates the value of Fahrenheit
   while the value Celsius is less than the value
   of the Upper_Limit. */
    while (Celsius  <= Upper_Limit) {
        Fahrenheit = Celsius * (9.0 / 5.0) + 32.0;

/* Display the table of data in floating point format. */
        printf("         %3.2f       %3.3f\n", Celsius,Fahrenheit);
        Celsius = Celsius + Step;
    }                            /* end of the "while" loop. */
}                                /* end of the main function. */
```

26

SET*.*: Printer Configuration Programs

The formatting capabilities of most, if not all, printers can be varied by sending appropriate control codes to them. This may be done by embedding the control codes in the files sent to the printers to be printed. It is not uncommon for default formatting conditions to be established by turning on or off dip switches. However, it is reasonable to assume that the default-setting dip switches of some of the printers are not readily accessible to the user, and not all conditions within the capability of the printer are brought out to dip switches.

This chapter is dedicated to menu driven programs that make it practicable to configure a printer directly from the keyboard and to return to the printer's default conditions by selecting the appropriate menu item.

We have included four programs for dot matrix printers. They are ready-made for the EPSON MX- and FX-series, the Fujitsu DPL-I 24-pin (which emulates the IBM Graphics Printer), the Siemens PT88 ink jet, and the SR-15 printer.

By noting the way the control codes are inserted in the source code for each of the printers you can customize any one of the four examples in this chapter to your specific printer, provided you know the control codes, which are usually given in the printer's documentation.

In Fig. 26-1, SETEPS, set up for the Epson, we have defined the control codes as plain English words or easily recognized partial words. In the subsequent programs we have not defined all the codes, but have used decimal identifiers inside the program. As an experiment you might try writing your own or defining the decimal statements at the start of the source code.

Fig. 26-1. Source code for SETEPS.

```
/* SETEPS - COPYRIGHT 1986 by T. O. Sidebottom/L. A. Wortman  */

/*     A configurator program for EPSON and other printers
       that use the same codes to control fonts.
*/

#include <stdio.h>

#define KEYBOARD_READ    7
#define COMPRESS        15
#define EMPHASIZE       69
#define DOUBLE_STRIKE   71
#define ELITE           77
#define ITALICS        180
#define RESET           64
#define ESC             27      /* Escape code       */
#define FORM_FEED       12
#define LINE_FEED       10
#define SKIP_PERF       78      /* Skip-perforations */
#define TOP_BOTTOM      12      /* Number of lines at bottom plus
                                   top of pages for skip-perf */
#define TRUE             1
#define PutPrinter(Ch)  putc(Ch,ListFile)
#define PRINTER         "prn"

main() {                        /* main */
    int     CurChar;
    FILE * ListFile;

 /* Display the menu. */
    printf("\n\n");
    printf("\t\t+-------------------------------------------------+\n");
    printf("\t\t|      EPSON-GRAFTRAX PRINTER-CONFIGURATOR        |\n");
    printf("\t\t+-------------------------------------------------+\n\n");
    printf("\t\tSelect one function at a time.  Functions may be\n");
    printf("\t\tcombined for special effects.  Type Y for RESET.\n\n");

    printf("\t\t--------------------FONTS------------------------\n");
    printf("\t\tA) Expanded (Continuous)        F) Double Strike\n");
    printf("\t\tB) Compressed                   G) Emphasized\n");
    printf("\t\tC) Elite                        H) Superscript\n");
    printf("\t\tD) Proportional                 I) Subscript\n");
    printf("\t\tE) Italics                      J) Underline\n\n");

    printf("\t\t--------------------PAPER------------------------\n");
    printf("\t\tK) Double Space                 M) Line Feed\n");
    printf("\t\tL) Single Space                 N) Form Feed\n");
    printf("\t\t                                O) Skip Perfs\n\n");

    printf("\t\t-------------------------------------------------\n");
    printf("\t\tX) TEST PRINT      Y) RESET      Z) RETURN TO DOS\n");
    printf("\t\t-------------------------------------------------\n\n");
```

```
   printf("\t\t(MSC 07-05-86)\7   CHOOSE A LETTER: ");

   freopen("con", "rb", stdin);

/* Open the ListFile. */
   if (!(ListFile = fopen(PRINTER, "w"))) {
       printf("Check the printer. Is it on? Plugged in?");
       exit(0);
   }

   while (TRUE) {

   /* Get the user's response from the keyboard. */
       CurChar = bdos(KEYBOARD_READ, 0) & 0x7F;

   /* Transmit the appropriate function code from the menu. */
       switch (CurChar) {
           case 'a':
           case 'A':
               PutPrinter(ESC);
               PutPrinter('W');
               PutPrinter(1);
               break;


           case 'b':
           case 'B':
               PutPrinter(COMPRESS);
               break;

           case 'c':
           case 'C':
               PutPrinter(ESC);
               PutPrinter(ELITE);
               break;

           case 'd':
           case 'D':
               PutPrinter(ESC);
               PutPrinter('p');
               PutPrinter(1);
               break;

           case 'e':
           case 'E':
               PutPrinter(ESC);
               PutPrinter(ITALICS);
               break;

           case 'f':
           case 'F':
               PutPrinter(ESC);
               PutPrinter(DOUBLE_STRIKE);
               break;
```

```
case 'g':
case 'G':
    PutPrinter(ESC);
    PutPrinter(EMPHASIZE);
    break;
case 'h':
case 'H':
    PutPrinter(ESC);
    PutPrinter('S');
    PutPrinter(0);
    break;

case 'i':
case 'I':
    PutPrinter(ESC);
    PutPrinter('S');
    PutPrinter(1);
    break;

case 'j':
case 'J':
    PutPrinter(ESC);
    PutPrinter('-');
    PutPrinter(1);
    break;

case 'k':
case 'K':
    PutPrinter(ESC);
    PutPrinter('A');
    PutPrinter(ESC);
    PutPrinter(36);
    break;

case 'l':
case 'L':
    PutPrinter(ESC);
    PutPrinter('2');
    break;

case 'm':
case 'M':
    PutPrinter(LINE_FEED);
    break;
case 'n':
case 'N':
    PutPrinter(FORM_FEED);
    break;

case 'o':
case 'O':
    PutPrinter(ESC);
    PutPrinter(SKIP_PERF);
    PutPrinter(TOP_BOTTOM);
    break;
```

```
    case 'x':
    case 'X':
        fprintf(ListFile, "ABCDEFGHIJKLMNOPQRSTUVWXYZ\n");
        fprintf(ListFile, "abcdefghijklmnopqrstuvwxyz\n");
        fprintf(ListFile, "01234567890-= !@#$%^&*()_+{}[]\n");
        fprintf(ListFile, "<>,.:;'?/|\~'*  END OF TEST\n\n");
        break;

    case 'y':
    case 'Y':
        PutPrinter(ESC);
        PutPrinter(64);
        break;

    case 'z':
    case 'Z':
        exit(0);

    default:            /* IF A WRONG KEY IS HIT */
    /* Display an error message. * Send the cursor back.  * Blank
       out (overwrite) the message.  * Send the cursor back. */
        printf("Wrong Key!\7");
        printf("\b\b\b\b\b\b\b\b\b\b\b");
        printf("           ");
        printf("\b\b\b\b\b\b\b\b\b\b\b");
}

    /* Display an error message for carriage returns. * Send the cursor
       back.  * Blank out (erase) the message.  * Send the cursor back. *
       Display the character that has been chosen. */
        if (CurChar == 0x0D) {
            printf("Do Not Press <CR>!\7");
            printf("\b\b\b\b\b\b\b\b\b\b\b\b\b\b\b\b\b\b");
            printf("                  ");
            printf("\b\b\b\b\b\b\b\b\b\b\b\b\b\b\b\b\b\b");
        }
        if (CurChar != 0x0D) {
            printf("%lc\b", CurChar);
        }

    /* Ring the printer's bell to confirm * transmission. */
        PutPrinter(7);

    /* Ensure the commands are immediately * sent to the printer by
       closing the * file to flush the buffer. */
        fflush(ListFile);
    }
}                               /* main */
```

Figure 26-2 is the menu displayed by SETEPS. Figure 26-3 is the source code for SETFUJI, and Fig. 26-4 is the menu displayed by SETFUJI. The source code for SETPT88 is Fig. 26-5, and Fig. 26-6 is the source code for SETSR15.

```
+-----------------------------------------------+
|       EPSON-GRAFTRAX PRINTER-CONFIGURATOR     |
+-----------------------------------------------+

Select one function at a time.  Functions may be
combined for special effects.  Type Y for RESET.

-------------------FONTS-----------------------
A) Expanded (Continuous)         F) Double Strike
B) Compressed                    G) Emphasized
C) Elite                         H) Superscript
D) Proportional                  I) Subscript
E) Italics                       J) Underline

-------------------PAPER-----------------------
K) Double Space                  M) Line Feed
L) Single Space                  N) Form Feed
                                 O) Skip Perfs

-----------------------------------------------
X) TEST PRINT      Y) RESET      Z) RETURN TO DOS
-----------------------------------------------

(MSC 07-05-86)   CHOOSE A LETTER:
```

Fig. 26-2. Menu display for SETEPS.

Fig. 26-3. Source code for SETFUJI.

```
/* SETFUJI - COPYRIGHT 1986 by T. O. Sidebottom/L. A. Wortman */

/*  A configurator program for FUJITSU DPL and other printers
    that use the same codes to control fonts in the IBM mode.
*/

#include <stdio.h>

#define KEYBOARD_READ     7
#define ESC              27
#define TRUE              1
#define PutPrinter(Ch)   putc(Ch,ListFile)
#define PRINTER          "prn"

main() {                          /* main */
    int     CurChar;
    FILE  *ListFile;
```

```
/* Display the menu. */
   printf("\n\n\n");
   printf("\t\t+---------------------------------------------+\n");
   printf("\t\t|        FUJITSU DPL-I PRINTER CONFIGURATOR       |\n");
   printf("\t\t|---------------------------------------------|\n");
   printf("\t\t| Select one letter at a time. Do not press <CR> |\n");
   printf("\t\t|---------------------------------------------|\n");
   printf("\t\t| A) Double-Width One-Line     M) Tiny Print     |\n");
   printf("\t\t| B) Double-Width Continuous   N) SPARE          |\n");
   printf("\t\t| C) Eighteen CPI (Compress)   O) Line Feed      |\n");
   printf("\t\t| D) Twelve CPI (Elite)        P) Form Feed      |\n");
   printf("\t\t| E) Ten CPI (Pica)            Q) Rev Line Feed  |\n");
   printf("\t\t| F) Proportional              R) Skipover Perf  |\n");
   printf("\t\t| G) Underline                 S) Auto Justify   |\n");
   printf("\t\t| H) Emphasized                T) Lft Margin 10  |\n");
   printf("\t\t| I) Double Strike             U) Lft Margin 20  |\n");
   printf("\t\t| J) Italics                   V) Lft Margin 30  |\n");
   printf("\t\t| K) Double Space (3-LPI)      W) Lft Margin 40  |\n");
   printf("\t\t| L) Single Space (6-LPI)      [MSC3 07-05-86]   |\n");
   printf("\t\t|---------------------------------------------|\n");
   printf("\t\t| X) TEST PRINT    Y) RESET    Z) RETURN TO DOS  |\n");
   printf("\t\t+---------------------------------------------+\n");
   printf("\n\t\t\7  CHOOSE A LETTER: ");

   freopen("con", "rb", stdin);

/* Open the ListFile. */
   if (!(ListFile = fopen(PRINTER, "w"))) {
       printf("Check the printer.  Is it on?  Plugged in?");
       exit(0);
   }

   while (TRUE) {

   /* Get the user's response from the keyboard. */
       CurChar = bdos(KEYBOARD_READ, 0) & 0x7F;

   /* Transmit the appropriate function code from the menu. */
       switch (CurChar) {
            case 'a':
            case 'A':           /* DOUBLE-WIDTH TO END OF LINE */
                PutPrinter(ESC);
                PutPrinter(14);
                break;

            case 'b':
            case 'B':           /* DOUBLE-WIDTH CONTINUOUS */
                PutPrinter(ESC);
                PutPrinter(87);
                PutPrinter(1);
                break;

            case 'c':
            case 'C':           /* COMPRESSED  18-CPI */
```

```
        PutPrinter(ESC);
        PutPrinter(15);
        break;
    case 'd':
    case 'D':           /* ELITE  12-CPI */
        PutPrinter(ESC);
        PutPrinter(77);
        break;

    case 'e':
    case 'E':           /* PICA  10-CPI */
        PutPrinter(ESC);
        PutPrinter(80);
        break;

    case 'f':
    case 'F':           /* PROPORTIONAL */
        PutPrinter(ESC);
        PutPrinter(112);
        PutPrinter(1);
        break;

    case 'g':
    case 'G':           /* UNDERLINE */
        PutPrinter(ESC);
        PutPrinter(45);
        PutPrinter(1);
        break;

    case 'h':
    case 'H':           /* EMPHASIZED */
        PutPrinter(ESC);
        PutPrinter(69);
        break;

    case 'i':
    case 'I':           /* DOUBLE STRIKE */
        PutPrinter(ESC);
        PutPrinter(71);
        break;
    case 'j':
    case 'J':           /* ITALICS */
        PutPrinter(ESC);
        PutPrinter(52);
        break;

    case 'k':
    case 'K':           /* DOUBLE SPACE */
        PutPrinter(ESC);
        PutPrinter('3');
        PutPrinter(60);
        break;

    case 'l':
    case 'L':           /* SINGLE SPACE */
```

```
        PutPrinter(ESC);
        PutPrinter('3');
        PutPrinter(30);
        break;

    case 'm':
    case 'M':           /* TINY PRINT */
        PutPrinter(ESC);
        PutPrinter('S');
        PutPrinter(1);
        PutPrinter(ESC);
        PutPrinter('3');
        PutPrinter(20);
        break;

    /* case 'n': case 'N':              -SPARE- */

    case 'o':
    case 'O':           /* LINE FEED */
        PutPrinter(10);
        break;
    case 'p':
    case 'P':           /* FORM FEED */
        PutPrinter(12);
        break;

    case 'q':
    case 'Q':           /* REVERSE LF */
        PutPrinter(ESC);
        PutPrinter(106);
        PutPrinter(30);
        break;

    case 'r':
    case 'R':           /* SKIP OVER PERFS */
        PutPrinter(ESC);
        PutPrinter(78);
        PutPrinter(12);
        break;

    case 's':
    case 'S':           /* AUTO JUSTIFY */
        PutPrinter(ESC);
        PutPrinter(109);
        break;

    case 't':
    case 'T':           /* LEFT MARGIN = 10 */
        PutPrinter(ESC);
        PutPrinter(108);
        PutPrinter(10);
        break;

    case 'u':
    case 'U':           /* LEFT MARGIN = 20 */
```

```
        PutPrinter(ESC);
        PutPrinter(108);
        PutPrinter(20);
        break;

    case 'v':
    case 'V':           /* LEFT MARGIN = 30 */
        PutPrinter(ESC);
        PutPrinter(108);
        PutPrinter(30);
        break;

    case 'w':
    case 'W':           /* LEFT MARGIN = 40 */
        PutPrinter(ESC);
        PutPrinter(108);
        PutPrinter(40);
        break;

    case 'x':
    case 'X':           /* TEST PRINT */
        fprintf(ListFile, "ABCDEFGHIJKLMNOPQRSTUVWXYZ\n");
        fprintf(ListFile, "abcdefghijklmnopqrstuvwxyz\n");
        fprintf(ListFile, "1234567890-=!@#$%^&*()_+<>\n");
        fprintf(ListFile, ":;,''./?\|[]{}~* End Of Test!\n\n");
        break;

    case 'y':
    case 'Y':           /* RESET PRINTER TO DEFAULT */
        PutPrinter(ESC);
        PutPrinter('@');
        break;

    case 'z':
    case 'Z':           /* RETURN TO DOS */
        exit(0);

    default:            /* IF A WRONG KEY IS HIT */
    /* Display an error message. * Send the cursor back.  * Blank
       out (overwrite) the message.  * Send the cursor back. */
        printf("Wrong Key!\7");
        printf("\b\b\b\b\b\b\b\b\b\b");
        printf("          ");
        printf("\b\b\b\b\b\b\b\b\b\b");
}

     /* Display an error message for carriage returns. * Send the cursor
        back.  * Blank out (erase) the message.  * Send the cursor back. *
        Display the character that has been chosen. */
         if (CurChar == 0x0D) {
             printf("Do Not Press <CR>!\7");
             printf("\b\b\b\b\b\b\b\b\b\b\b\b\b\b\b\b\b\b");
             printf("                  ");
             printf("\b\b\b\b\b\b\b\b\b\b\b\b\b\b\b\b\b\b");
         }
         if (CurChar != 0x0D) {
```

```
            printf("%lc\b", CurChar);
        }

    /* Ring the printer's bell to confirm * transmission. */
        PutPrinter(7);

    /* Ensure the commands are immediately * sent to the printer by
       closing the * file to flush the buffer. */
        fflush(ListFile);
    }
}                                   /* main */
```

```
+----------------------------------------------------+
|          FUJITSU DPL-I PRINTER CONFIGURATOR         |
|----------------------------------------------------|
| Select one letter at a time. Do not press <CR>     |
|----------------------------------------------------|
| A) Double-Width One-Line       M) Tiny Print        |
| B) Double-Width Continuous     N) SPARE             |
| C) Eighteen CPI (Compress)     O) Line Feed         |
| D) Twelve CPI (Elite)          P) Form Feed         |
| E) Ten CPI (Pica)              Q) Rev Line Feed     |
| F) Proportional                R) Skipover Perf     |
| G) Underline                   S) Auto Justify      |
| H) Emphasized                  T) Lft Margin 10     |
| I) Double Strike               U) Lft Margin 20     |
| J) Italics                     V) Lft Margin 30     |
| K) Double Space (3-LPI)        W) Lft Margin 40     |
| L) Single Space (6-LPI)        [MSC3 07-05-86]      |
|----------------------------------------------------|
| X) TEST PRINT    Y) RESET     Z) RETURN TO DOS     |
+----------------------------------------------------+

  CHOOSE A LETTER:
```

Fig. 26-4. Menu display for SETFUJI.

Fig. 26-5. Source code for SETPT88.

```
/* SETPT88.C - COPYRIGHT 1986 by T. O. Sidebottom/L. A. Wortman */

/* A configurator program for SIEMENS PT88 and other printers
   that use the same codes to control fonts in the IBM mode.
*/

#include <stdio.h>
```

```
#define KEYBOARD_READ    7
#define ESC             27
#define TRUE             1
#define PutPrinter(Ch)  putc(Ch,ListFile)
#define PRINTER         "prn"

main()
{   /* main */
        int             CurChar ;
        FILE        *ListFile ;

        /* Display the menu. */
        printf("\n\n\n") ;
        printf("\t\t+-----------------------------------------------+\n") ;
        printf("\t\t|       SIEMENS-PT88    PRINTER-CONFIGURATOR      |\n") ;
        printf("\t\t|-----------------------------------------------|\n") ;
        printf("\t\t| Select one letter at a time. Do not press <CR> |\n") ;
        printf("\t\t|-----------------------------------------------|\n") ;
        printf("\t\t| A) One-Line Wide Pitch        M) OFF           |\n") ;
        printf("\t\t| B) Continuous Wide Pitch      N) OFF           |\n") ;
        printf("\t\t| C) Narrow Pitch (17 CPI)      O) OFF           |\n") ;
        printf("\t\t| D) Elite Pitch  (12 CPI)      P) OFF           |\n") ;
        printf("\t\t| E) Pica Pitch   (10 CPI)      Q) OFF           |\n") ;
        printf("\t\t| F) Skip Perforations          R) OFF           |\n") ;
        printf("\t\t| G) Underline                  S) OFF           |\n") ;
        printf("\t\t| H) Bold Printing              T) OFF           |\n") ;
        printf("\t\t| I) Emphasized Printing        U) OFF           |\n") ;
        printf("\t\t| J) SPARE                      V) Line Feed     |\n") ;
        printf("\t\t| K) Double Space (3 LPI)       W) Form Feed     |\n") ;
        printf("\t\t| L) Single Space (6 LPI)       X) SPARE         |\n") ;
        printf("\t\t|-----------------------------------------------|\n") ;
        printf("\t\t| Y) TEST PRINT                 Z) RETURN TO DOS |\n") ;
        printf("\t\t+-----------------------------------------------+\n") ;
        printf("\n\t\t[MSC 07-05-86]\t\7CHOOSE A LETTER: ") ;

        freopen("con","rb","stdin") ;

        /* Open the ListFile. */
        if (!(ListFile = fopen(PRINTER,"w"))) {
                printf("Can't access the printer. Please check it!") ;
                exit(0) ;
        }

        while (TRUE) {

                /* Get the user's response from the keyboard. */
                CurChar = bdos(KEYBOARD_READ,0) & 0x7F ;

                /* Transmit the appropriate function code from the menu. */
                switch(CurChar) {
                case 'a':
                case 'A':       /* WIDE TO END OF LINE */
                        PutPrinter(14) ;
                        break ;
```

```
case 'b':
case 'B':       /* WIDE CONTINUOUSLY */
        PutPrinter(27) ;
        PutPrinter(87) ;
        PutPrinter(49) ;
        break ;

case 'c':
case 'C':               /* NARROW (17 CPI) */
        PutPrinter(15) ;
        break ;
case 'd':
case 'D':               /* ELITE (12 CPI) */
        PutPrinter(ESC) ;
        PutPrinter(91) ;
        PutPrinter(50) ;
        PutPrinter(119) ;
        break ;

case 'e':
case 'E':               /* PICA (10 CPI) */
        PutPrinter(ESC) ;
        PutPrinter(91) ;
        PutPrinter(49) ;
        PutPrinter(119) ;
        break ;

case 'f':
case 'F':               /* SKIP OVER PERFORATIONS */
        PutPrinter(ESC) ;
        PutPrinter(78) ;
        PutPrinter(12) ;
        break ;

case 'g':
case 'G':               /* UNDERLINE */
        PutPrinter(ESC) ;
        PutPrinter(45) ;
        PutPrinter(1) ;
        break ;

case 'h':
case 'H':               /* BOLD PRINTING */
        PutPrinter(ESC) ;
        PutPrinter(71) ;
        break ;
case 'i':
case 'I':               /* EMPHASIZED PRINTING */
        PutPrinter(ESC) ;
        PutPrinter(69) ;
        break ;

case 'j':
case 'J':               /* SPARE */
```

```
        break ;

case 'k':
case 'K':                /* DOUBLE SPACE */
        PutPrinter(ESC) ;
        PutPrinter('A') ;
        PutPrinter(24) ;
        PutPrinter(ESC) ;
        PutPrinter('2') ;
        break ;

case 'l':
case 'L':                /* SINGLE SPACE */
        PutPrinter(ESC) ;
        PutPrinter('A') ;
        PutPrinter(12) ;
        PutPrinter(ESC) ;
        PutPrinter('2') ;
        break ;

case 'm':
case 'M' :       /* ONE-LINE WIDE PRINT OFF */
        PutPrinter(20) ;
        break ;

case 'n':
case 'N':                /* CONTINUOUS WIDE PRINT OFF */
        PutPrinter(ESC) ;
        PutPrinter(87) ;
        PutPrinter(48) ;
        break ;

case 'o':
case 'O':                /* CANCEL NARROW PITCH */
        PutPrinter(18) ;
        break ;

case 'p':
case 'P':                /* CANCEL ELITE */
        PutPrinter(27) ;
        break ;

case 'q':
case 'Q':                /* CANCEL PICA */
        PutPrinter(27) ;
        break ;

case 'r':
case 'R':        /* DEACTIVATE SKIP OVER PERFS */
        PutPrinter(ESC) ;
        PutPrinter('O') ;
        break ;

case 's':
case 'S':                /* UNDERLINE OFF */
```

```
            PutPrinter(ESC) ;
            PutPrinter(45) ;
            PutPrinter(0) ;
            break ;

    case 't':
    case 'T':                 /* BOLD PRINTING OFF */
            PutPrinter(ESC) ;
            PutPrinter(72) ;
            break ;

    case 'u':
    case 'U':                 /* EMPHASIZED PRINTING OFF */
            PutPrinter(ESC) ;
            PutPrinter(70) ;
            break ;
    case 'v':
    case 'V':         /* LINE FEED */
            PutPrinter(10) ;
            break ;

    case 'w':
    case 'W':           /* FORM FEED */
            PutPrinter(12) ;
            break ;

    case 'x' :
    case 'X':          /* SPARE */
            break ;

    case 'y':
    case 'Y':                 /* TEST PRINT */
            fprintf(ListFile,"ABCDEFGHIJKLMNOPQRSTUVWXYZ\n") ;
            fprintf(ListFile,"abcdefghijklmnopqrstuvwxyz\n") ;
            fprintf(ListFile,"1234567890-=!@#$%^&*()_+<>\n") ;
            fprintf(ListFile,":;,''./?\|[]{}~* End Of Test!\n\n") ;
            break ;

    case 'z':
    case 'Z':           /* RETURN TO DOS */
            exit(0) ;

    default:
            /* If a no-case key is hit:       */
            /* Display an error message when  */
            /* a no-case key is hit.          */
            /* Then send the cursor back.     */
            /* Blank out (erase) the message. */
            /* Send the cursor back.          */

            printf("Wrong Key!\7") ;
            printf("\b\b\b\b\b\b\b\b\b\b\b") ;
            printf("           ") ;
            printf("\b\b\b\b\b\b\b\b\b\b\b") ;
    }
```

```
                /* Display an error message for carriage returns. */
                /* Send the cursor back.                          */
                /* Blank out (erase) the message.                 */
                /* Send the cursor back.                          */
                /* Display the character that has been chosen.    */

                if(CurChar == 0x0D) {
                        printf("Do Not Press <CR>!\7") ;
                        printf("\b\b\b\b\b\b\b\b\b\b\b\b\b\b\b\b\b\b") ;
                        printf("                  ") ;
                        printf("\b\b\b\b\b\b\b\b\b\b\b\b\b\b\b\b\b\b") ;
                }
                if(CurChar != 0x0D) {
                        printf("%1s\b",&CurChar) ;
                }

                /* Ring the printer's bell to confirm transmission. */
                PutPrinter(7) ;

                /* Ensure the commands are immediately */
                /* sent to the printer by flushing the */
                /* the buffer.                         */
                fflush(ListFile) ;
        }
} /* end of main */
```

Fig. 26-6. Source code for SETSR15.

```
/* SETSR15 - COPYRIGHT 1986 by T. O. Sidebottom/L. A. Wortman  */

/*  A configurator program for STAR-15 and other printers that
    use the same codes to control fonts in the IBM mode.
*/

#include <stdio.h>

#define KEYBOARD_READ    7
#define ESC             27
#define TRUE             1
#define PutPrinter(Ch)  putc(Ch,ListFile)
#define PRINTER         "prn"

main()
{   /* main */
        int     CurChar ;
        FILE    *ListFile ;

        /* Display the menu.  */
        printf("\n\n\n") ;
        printf("\t\t+----------------------------------------------+\n") ;
        printf("\t\t|        STAR SR15 PC-PRINTER CONFIGURATOR      |\n") ;
```

```
printf("\t\t|-----------------------------------------------|\n") ;
printf("\t\t| Select one letter at a time. Do not press <CR> |\n") ;
printf("\t\t|-----------------------------------------------|\n") ;
printf("\t\t| A) One-Line Expanded          M) Tiny Print    |\n") ;
printf("\t\t| B) Continuous Expanded        N) SPARE         |\n") ;
printf("\t\t| C) Seventeen CPI              O) Line Feed     |\n") ;
printf("\t\t| D) Twelve CPI (Elite)         P) Form Feed     |\n") ;
printf("\t\t| E) Ten CPI (Pica)             Q) Rev Form Feed |\n") ;
printf("\t\t| F) Proportional               R) Btm Margin 12 |\n") ;
printf("\t\t| G) Underline                  S) Cut Sheet Feed |\n") ;
printf("\t\t| H) Emphasized                 T) Lft Margin 10 |\n") ;
printf("\t\t| I) Double Strike              U) Lft Margin 20 |\n") ;
printf("\t\t| J) Near Letter Quality        V) Lft Margin 30 |\n") ;
printf("\t\t| K) Double Space (3-LPI)       W) Lft Margin 40 |\n") ;
printf("\t\t| L) Single Space (6-LPI)        [MSC  07-05-86] |\n") ;
printf("\t\t|-----------------------------------------------|\n") ;
printf("\t\t| X) TEST PRINT    Y) RESET    Z) RETURN TO DOS  |\n") ;
printf("\t\t+-----------------------------------------------+\n") ;
printf("\n\t\t\7  CHOOSE A LETTER: ") ;

freopen("con","rb",stdin) ;

/* Open the ListFile. */
if (!(ListFile = fopen(PRINTER,"w"))) {
        printf("Check the Printer, Please!") ;
        exit(0) ;
}

while (TRUE) {

        /* Get the user's response from the keyboard.
                 */
        CurChar = bdos(KEYBOARD_READ,0) & 0x7F ;

        /* Transmit the appropriate function code from the menu. */
        switch(CurChar) {
        case 'a':
        case 'A':           /* EXPAND TO END OF LINE */
                PutPrinter(ESC) ;
                PutPrinter(14) ;
                break ;

        case 'b':
        case 'B':           /* EXPAND CONTINUOUSLY */
                PutPrinter(ESC) ;
                PutPrinter('W') ;
                PutPrinter(1) ;
                break ;
        case 'c':
        case 'C':           /* COMPRESSED  17-CPI */
                PutPrinter(ESC) ;
                PutPrinter(15) ;
                break ;

        case 'd':
```

```
case 'D':          /* ELITE  12-CPI */
        PutPrinter(ESC) ;
        PutPrinter(77) ;
        break ;

case 'e':
case 'E':          /* PICA  10-CPI */
        PutPrinter(ESC) ;
        PutPrinter(' ') ;
        break ;

case 'f':
case 'F':          /* PROPORTIONAL */
        PutPrinter(ESC) ;
        PutPrinter('p') ;
        PutPrinter(1) ;
        break ;

case 'g':
case 'G':          /* UNDERLINE */
        PutPrinter(ESC) ;
        PutPrinter('-') ;
        PutPrinter(1) ;
        break ;

case 'h':
case 'H':          /* EMPHASIZED */
        PutPrinter(ESC) ;
        PutPrinter(69) ;
        break ;
case 'i':
case 'I':          /* DOUBLE STRIKE */
        PutPrinter(ESC) ;
        PutPrinter(71) ;
        break ;



case 'j':
case 'J':          /* NEAR LETTER QUALITY */
        PutPrinter(ESC) ;
        PutPrinter(52) ;
        break ;

case 'k':
case 'K':          /* DOUBLE SPACE */
        PutPrinter(ESC) ;
        PutPrinter('A') ;
        PutPrinter(24) ;
        PutPrinter(ESC) ;
        PutPrinter('2') ;
        break ;

case 'l':
case 'L':          /* SINGLE SPACE */
```

```
        PutPrinter(ESC) ;
        PutPrinter('A') ;
        PutPrinter(12) ;
        PutPrinter(ESC) ;
        PutPrinter('2') ;
        break ;

case 'm':
case 'M' :        /* TINY PRINT */
        PutPrinter(ESC) ;
        PutPrinter('A') ;
        PutPrinter(6) ;
        PutPrinter(ESC) ;
        PutPrinter('2') ;
        PutPrinter(ESC) ;
        PutPrinter('S') ;
        PutPrinter(1) ;
        break ;

case 'n':
case 'N': /* PAGE LENGTH 90 LINES - CUT SHEET */
        PutPrinter(ESC) ;  /* Set page length */
        PutPrinter('C') ;  /* 90 lines.       */
        PutPrinter(90) ;
        PutPrinter('O') ;  /* Cancel top and  */
        PutPrinter(ESC) ;  /* bottom margins. */
        PutPrinter('r') ;  /* Set top margin  */
        PutPrinter(0) ;    /* to zero.        */
        PutPrinter(ESC) ;  /* Set bottom      */
        PutPrinter('N') ;  /* to 32 lines.    */
        PutPrinter(32) ;
        break ;

case 'o':
case 'O':         /* LINE FEED */
        PutPrinter(10) ;
        break ;

case 'p':
case 'P':         /* FORM FEED */
        PutPrinter(12) ;
        break ;

case 'q':
case 'Q':         /* REVERSE FF AFTER LINE FEEDS*/
        PutPrinter(0x1B) ;
        PutPrinter(0x0C) ;
        break ;

case 'r':
case 'R':         /* BOTTOM MARGIN = 12 */
        PutPrinter(ESC) ;
        PutPrinter(78) ;
        PutPrinter(12) ;
        break ;
```

```
case 's':
case 'S':  /* CUT SHEET - 90 LINES PER PAGE */
        PutPrinter(ESC) ;
        PutPrinter('C') ;
        PutPrinter(90) ;
        PutPrinter(ESC) ;
        PutPrinter('N') ;
        PutPrinter(32) ;
        break ;

case 't':
case 'T':           /* LEFT MARGIN = 10 */
        PutPrinter(ESC) ;
        PutPrinter(108) ;
        PutPrinter(10) ;
        break ;

case 'u':
case 'U':           /* LEFT MARGIN = 20 */
        PutPrinter(ESC) ;
        PutPrinter(108) ;
        PutPrinter(20) ;
        break ;

case 'v':
case 'V':           /* LEFT MARGIN = 30 */
        PutPrinter(ESC) ;
        PutPrinter(108) ;
        PutPrinter(30) ;
        break ;

case 'w':
case 'W':           /* LEFT MARGIN = 40 */
        PutPrinter(ESC) ;
        PutPrinter(108) ;
        PutPrinter(40) ;
        break ;

case 'x':
case 'X':           /* TEST PRINT */
        fprintf(ListFile,"ABCDEFGHIJKLMNOPQRSTUVWXYZ\n") ;
        fprintf(ListFile,"abcdefghijklmnopqrstuvwxyz\n") ;
        fprintf(ListFile,"1234567890-=!@#$%^&*()_+<>\n") ;
        fprintf(ListFile,":;,''./?\|[]{}~* End Of Test!\n\n") ;
        break ;

case 'y':
case 'Y':           /* RESET PRINTER TO DEFAULT */
        PutPrinter(ESC) ;
        PutPrinter('@') ;
        break ;

case 'z':
case 'Z':           /* RETURN TO DOS */
        exit(0) ;
```

```
default:                        /* IF A WRONG KEY IS HIT */
        /* Display an error message when a wrong key is hit.
                     * Send the cursor back.
                     * Blank out (erase) the message.
                     * Send the cursor back.
                     */
        printf("Wrong Key!\7") ;
        printf("\b\b\b\b\b\b\b\b\b\b") ;
        printf("          ") ;
        printf("\b\b\b\b\b\b\b\b\b\b") ;
}

/* Display an error message for carriage returns.
            * Send the cursor back.
            * Blank out (erase) the message.
            * Send the cursor back.
            * Display the character that has been chosen.
            */
if(CurChar == 0x0D) {
        printf("Do Not Press <CR>!\7") ;
        printf("\b\b\b\b\b\b\b\b\b\b\b\b\b\b\b\b\b\b") ;
        printf("                  ") ;
                        printf("\b\b\b\b\b\b\b\b\b\b\b\b\b\b\b\b\b\b") ;
                }

                if(CurChar != 0x0D) {
                        printf("%lc\b",CurChar) ;
                }

                /* Ring the printer's bell to confirm
                         * transmission.
                         */
                PutPrinter(7) ;

                /* Ensure the commands are immediately
                         * sent to the printer by closing the
                         * file to flush the buffer.
                         */
                fflush(ListFile) ;
        }
}  /* main */
```

27

DUPOUT: Remove Duplicate Lines

The value, utility, and usage of the DUPOUT program, Fig. 27-1, is concisely stated in the opening comment built into its source code:

> "DUPOUT removes duplicate lines from an ASCII text file. Duplicate lines can arise by merging two text files together where some lines are the same. Rather than removing duplicates by hand, DUPOUT removes them automatically. It removes duplicates that are adjacent to each other, so sort the text file before removing duplicates.
>
> To use DUPOUT, type:

dupout ***filename*** **[>*output file*]**

where filename is the name of the file to process. Optionally, you may place the output in a file by using the right angle bracket redirection symbol and the name of the output file.

Fig. 27-1. Source code for DUPOUT.

```
/* Dupout removes duplicate lines from an ASCII text file. Duplicate
lines can arise by merging two text files together where some lines
are the same. Rather than removing duplicates by hand, dupout
removes them automatically. It removes duplicates that are adjacent
to each other, so sort the text file before removing duplicates.

To use dupout, type

            dupout  filename  [>output file]

where filename is the name of the file to process. Optionally you
may place the output in a file by using the right angle bracket
redirection symbol, and the name of the output file. */


/* Include files
 */
#include <stdio.h>

/* Definitions
 */
#define EOS '\0'
#define MAXSTRLEN 255

main(argc, argv)
int     argc;
char   *argv[];
{                               /* main */
    int     Current = 1;
    FILE * InputFile = stdin;
    char    CompareText[2][MAXSTRLEN];

    if ((argc >= 2) &&
            ((InputFile = fopen(argv[1], "r")) == (FILE *) NULL)) {
        fprintf(stderr, "Unable to open input file: %s.", argv[1]);
        exit(0);
    }

    *CompareText[0] = EOS;

    while (fgets(CompareText[Current], MAXSTRLEN, InputFile)
            != (char *) NULL) {
        if (strcmp(CompareText[Current], CompareText[1 - Current]) != 0) {
            fputs(CompareText[Current], stdout);

        /* Toggle Current between 0 and 1. */
            Current = 1 - Current;
        }
    }
}                               /* main */
```

28

MAXSORT: Sorting Very Large Files

This is a powerful and complex program. Whether or not you have an immediate need for a program of such unusual capabilities as MAXSORT embodies, (Fig. 28-1) study the code, its structure, and numerous calls to functions. This program may be used to sort ASCII files prior to deleting duplicate lines of text with the DUPOUT program in Chapter 27.

The code is unusually heavy with comments to help you learn precisely what is happening throughout the program. When the code is commented in this way there is little that can be added by preliminary text.

Therefore, consider that the code supports the tutorial and will probably provide answers that preclude any additional questions. Remember, too, that the compiler ignores comments; they do not add to the length of the executable program.

Fig. 28-1. Source code for MAXSORT.

```
/* Maxsort is a sorting program that can sort text files too large to
fit into memory. It does so by breaking the file into pieces, called
runs, and then reassembling the sorted runs into the final file. The
program handles the breakage and reassembly automatically.

To use maxsort, enter:

           maxsort  filename  [output file]

where filename is the name of the file to sort. Optionally you
may put the sorted output in a file by putting the output file
name to create at the end of the command line. */

/* Include files
 */
#include <stdio.h>
#include <malloc.h>

/* Definitions
 */
#define min(a,b) ((a < b) ? a : b)

#define BOOL int
#define BUFFERSIZE 20000          /* This variable controls the size of the
                                     buffer to sort. Vary this parameter
                                     with the size of memory. */
#define CTRLZ 26
#define EOS '\0'
#define FILENAMELEN 20
#define MAXSTRLEN 255
#define MAXNUMLINES      1000
#define MERGEORDER       3
#define TEMPFILEEND      ".TMP"
#define TEMPFILESTART    "S"
/* Global variables
 */
FILE * InFile;                    /* master input file */
int     Lines[MAXNUMLINES];       /* pointers to the beginning of lines in
                                     Buffer */
FILE * MergeFiles[MERGEORDER];    /* MERGEORDER files are opened
                                     simultaneously for merging.  */
int     NextBufAvail = 0;         /* marks the next available position in
                                     Buffer */
int     NextLine = 0;             /* marks the next available position in
                                     Lines */
int     NextMergeFile = 0;        /* marks the next available posiiton in
                                     MergeFiles */
int     SortNumber = 0;

/* Forward declarations
 */
int     CompareStrings();
```

```
BOOL GetSortBuffer();
void MakeFileName();
void Merge();
void OpenMergeInput();
FILE * OpenOutFile();
void ResortMergeBuffer();
void RemoveFiles();
void SortBuffer();
void WriteLines();


main(argc, argv)
int     argc;
char   *argv[];
{                               /* main */
    char   *Buffer;             /* Pointer to allocated buffer. */
    BOOL ContinueReading;
    int     Limit;
    int     MergeIndex;
    FILE * OutFile;             /* Output file */
    char    OutputFileName[FILENAMELEN];

InFile = stdin;
OutputFileName[0] = EOS;

/* Parse the command line. If there is a first argument, open that name
   as the input file. If there is a second argument, open it as an output
   file. If an argument is missing, leave it open to standard input or
   output. */
if ((argc > 1) &&
        ((InFile = fopen(argv[1], "r")) == (FILE *) NULL)) {
    fprintf(stderr, "Unable to open %s for input.",
            argv[1]);
    exit(0);
}

if (argc > 2)
    strcpy(OutputFileName, argv[2]);

/* Allocate the Buffer. Buffer is a pointer to the area where we store
   the lines to sort. Adjust the BUFFERSIZE constant depending on your
   computer's memory size. */
Buffer = malloc(BUFFERSIZE);

/* Sort runs. For each run, get a buffer-full of data. This may be less
   than the complete file, so we sort this amount of data (called a run),
   and write it to an output file. This process continues untill
   GetSortBuffer returns FALSE, indicating that we have read the entire
   input file. */
do {
    ContinueReading = GetSortBuffer(Buffer);
    OutFile = OpenOutFile(NextMergeFile++);
    SortBuffer(Buffer, Lines, NextLine);
    WriteLines(OutFile, Buffer);
    if (fclose(OutFile) != NULL) {
```

```
            fprintf(stderr, "Unable to close merge file.");
            exit(0);
        }
        fprintf(stderr, "Sort run completed.\n");
    } while (ContinueReading);
    if (fclose(InFile) != NULL) {
        fprintf(stderr, "Unable to close input file.");
        exit(0);
    }
/* With sorting complete, we no longer need Buffer. We free it, returning
    memory to the active memory pool. */
    free(Buffer);

/* We now have runs of data on the disk which we must merge back together
    into the final sorted file. This loop opens MERGEORDER files at a
    time, and merges these files into another run, three times longer than
    the input runs. This process continues, progressively building up
    larger merge runs, until we have the entire sorted file. This is
    called the sort-merge strategy for sorting files larger than will fit
    in available memory. */
    for (MergeIndex = 0; (MergeIndex < (NextMergeFile - 1));
            (MergeIndex += MERGEORDER)) {
        Limit = min(MergeIndex + MERGEORDER, NextMergeFile);
        OpenMergeInput(MergeIndex, Limit);
        OutFile = OpenOutFile(NextMergeFile++);
        Merge(MergeFiles, OutFile, Limit - MergeIndex);
        if (fclose(OutFile) != NULL) {
            fprintf(stderr, "Unable to close merge file.");
            exit(0);
        }
        RemoveFiles(MergeFiles, MergeIndex, Limit);
        fprintf(stderr, "Merge run completed.\n");
    }

/* We now have a temporary file with the final output. If we're
    generating another disk-resident file, we simply rename the file. If
    not, we must copy the file to the output stream--stdout. */
    if (OutputFileName[0] != EOS) {
        char    TmpFileName[FILENAMELEN];

        MakeFileName(--NextMergeFile, TmpFileName);
        unlink(OutputFileName); /* Ignore return value. */
        if (rename(TmpFileName, OutputFileName) != NULL) {
            fprintf(stderr, "Unable to use output file.");
            exit(0);

        }
    }
    else
        CopyToDestination(--NextMergeFile);
}                                   /* main */


/* CompareStrings compares String1 and String2, assumed to terminate
    with EOS. To do more complex sorting, add additional code to compare
```

```
   the strings here. For example, one could do a sort in inverse order
   by changing this function. Like strcmp itself, CompareStrings returns
   zero if the strings are equal; a value greater than zero if the first
   string is greater than the second string (using the ASCII collating
   sequence); or less than zero if the first string is less than the
   second string. */
int     CompareStrings(String1, String2)
char   *String1;
char   *String2;
{                                   /* CompareStrings */
    return(strcmp(String1, String2));
}                                   /* CompareStrings */

/* CopyToDestination opens the finalmerge run, writes its
   content to standard output, and then closes both files. */
CopyToDestination(FileNum)
int     FileNum;
{                                   /* CopyToDestination */
    FILE * FilePtr;
    char    FileName[FILENAMELEN];
    char    Line[MAXSTRLEN];
    int     Value;

    MakeFileName(FileNum, FileName);
    if ((FilePtr = fopen(FileName, "r")) == (FILE *) NULL) {
        fprintf(stderr, "Error in reopening final merge file.");
        exit(0);
    }
 /* Copy the file to stdout. */
    while (fgets(Line, MAXSTRLEN, FilePtr) != (char *) NULL)
        fputs(Line, stdout);
    if (fclose(stdout) != NULL) {
        fprintf(stderr, "Unable to close output file.");
        exit(0);
    }

    if (fclose(FilePtr) != NULL) {
        fprintf(stderr, "Unable to close merge file.");
        exit(0);
    }
    unlink(FileName);
}                                   /* CopyToDestination */


/* GetSortBuffer fills Buffer with characters from the input stream
   until EOF is reached or Buffer is completely filled. Note that each
   line has a Lines index set to point to it. GetSortBuffer returns TRUE
   if end-of-file or an error occurs; otherwise FALSE is returned. */
BOOL GetSortBuffer(Buffer)
char   *Buffer;
{                                   /* GetSortBuffer */
    int     CurChar;

    NextBufAvail = 0;
    NextLine = 0;
```

```
    Lines[0] = 0;                 /* zeroth entry is never used */

 /* Transfer characters into Buffer until EOF or an error is reached. */
    while (((CurChar = getc(InFile)) != EOF) && (CurChar != CTRLZ)) {
        Buffer[NextBufAvail++] = CurChar;

        if (CurChar == '\n') {
        /* If the end of line is reached, terminate the line entry and set
           the next Lines pointer to the next location in Buffer. The
           newline character is suppressed to not affect the sort
           ordering. */
            Buffer[NextBufAvail - 1] = EOS;/* zap newline */
            Lines[++NextLine] = NextBufAvail;

        /* If the Lines array is full or if Buffer is within one lineful
           of being completely full, exit. */
            if ((NextLine >= MAXNUMLINES) ||
                    (NextBufAvail > (BUFFERSIZE - MAXSTRLEN)))
                break;
        }
    }

 /* For the last line, add a line terminator. */
    Buffer[NextBufAvail - 1] = EOS;

    return(CurChar != EOF);
}                               /* GetSortBuffer */

/* MakeFileName returns a filename of form "XXXXXxxx.XXX", where xxx
   is the ASCII equivalent of FileNum. */
void MakeFileName(FileNum, Destination)
int     FileNum;
char    Destination[];
{                               /* MakeFileName */
    char    NumBuffer[10];

    Destination[0] = EOS;
    strcat(Destination, TEMPFILESTART);
    sprintf(NumBuffer, "%d", FileNum);
    if (strlen(NumBuffer) > (8 - strlen(TEMPFILESTART))) {
        fprintf(stderr, "Too many merge files.");
        exit(0);
    }
    strcat(Destination, NumBuffer);
    strcat(Destination, TEMPFILEEND);
}                               /* MakeFileName */

/* Merge merges input from the MergeFiles into OutFile.  A MERGEORDER-th
   way balanced merge is used.  One line from each of NumFiles files is
   first stored in the local buffer MergeBuf.  This is then sorted and the
   merge begins. */
void Merge(MergeFiles, OutFile, NumFiles)
FILE * MergeFiles[];
int     NumFiles;
FILE * OutFile;
{                               /* Merge */
```

```
   char    MergeBuf[MERGEORDER * MAXSTRLEN];
/* MergeBuf is NOT a two-dimensional array since it is passed to
   SortBuffer (which is also called elsewhere), which expects a
   one-dimensional array. */
   int     MergeLines[MERGEORDER];
   int     I,
           J;

/* Read one line from each file, just to get the ball rolling. */
   for (I = 0, J = 0; (I < NumFiles); I++, J += MAXSTRLEN) {
       MergeLines[I] = J;
       fgets(&MergeBuf[J], MAXSTRLEN, MergeFiles[I]);
   }

   SortBuffer(MergeBuf, MergeLines, NumFiles);

   while (NumFiles > 0) {
   /* Write the lowest string in the MergeBuf heap. */
       fputs(&MergeBuf[MergeLines[0]], OutFile);

   /* Replace the line just written with another from the same file. */
       if (fgets(&MergeBuf[MergeLines[0]], MAXSTRLEN,
                   MergeFiles[MergeLines[0] / MAXSTRLEN])
               == (char *) NULL) {
       /* We have exhausted one of the files. */
       /* Rearrange MergeLines and reduce NumFiles by one. */
           MergeLines[0] = MergeLines[--NumFiles];
       }
       ResortMergeBuffer(MergeBuf, MergeLines, NumFiles);
   }
                                  /* Merge */
/* OpenMergeInput opens files starting with Start and ending with Stop,
   where these numbers are used to form the filenames. */
void OpenMergeInput(Start, Stop)
int      Start,
         Stop;
{                                 /* OpenMergeInput */
    int      I;
    char     FileName[FILENAMELEN];
    int      Range = Stop - Start;

    if (Range > MERGEORDER) {
        fprintf(stderr,
                "Internal error.");
        exit(0);
    }

    for (I = 0; (I < Range); I++) {
        MakeFileName(Start + I, FileName);
        if ((MergeFiles[I] = fopen(FileName, "r")) == (FILE *) NULL) {
            fprintf(stderr, "Error in reopening merge file.");
            exit(0);
        }
    }
}                                 /* OpenMergeInput */
```

```
/* OpenOutFile opens a temporary output file. */
FILE * OpenOutFile(FileNum)
int     FileNum;
{                               /* OpenOutFile */
    FILE * FilePtr;
    char    FileName[FILENAMELEN];

    MakeFileName(FileNum, FileName);
    if ((FilePtr = fopen(FileName, "w")) == (FILE *) NULL) {
        fprintf(stderr, "Error in opening merge file.");
        exit(0);
    }
    return(FilePtr);
}                               /* OpenOutFile */

/* ResortMergeBuffer rearranges the values of MergeLines so that
   MergeLines[0] is pointing to the line with the smallest collating
   value. */
void ResortMergeBuffer(MergeBuf, MergeLines, NumFiles)
char    MergeBuf[];
int     MergeLines[];
int     NumFiles;
{                               /* ResortMergeBuffer */

    register int    I = 0;
    register int    J = 1 /* 2*I + 1 */ ;
    int     Temp;

    while (J < NumFiles) {
        if (J < (NumFiles - 1))
            if (CompareStrings(&MergeBuf[MergeLines[J]],
                        &MergeBuf[MergeLines[J + 1]]) > 0)
                J++;
        if (CompareStrings(&MergeBuf[MergeLines[I]],
                    &MergeBuf[MergeLines[J]]) <= 0)
            break;
        Temp = MergeLines[J];
        MergeLines[J] = MergeLines[I];
        MergeLines[I] = Temp;
        I = J;
        J = I + I /* 2*I */ ;
    }
}                               /* ResortMergeBuffer */


/* RemoveFiles removes MergeFiles corresponding to Start thru Stop. */
void RemoveFiles(MergeFiles, Start, Stop)
FILE * MergeFiles[];
int     Start;
int     Stop;
{
    char    FileName[FILENAMELEN];
    register int    I;
    register int    Range = Stop - Start;

        if (Range > MERGEORDER) {
```

```
        fprintf(stderr,
                "Internal error.");
        exit(0);
    }

    for (I = 0; (I < Range); I++) {
        MakeFileName(Start + I, FileName);
        if (fclose(MergeFiles[I]) != NULL) {
            fprintf(stderr, "Unable to close merge file.");
            exit(0);
        }
        unlink(FileName);
    }
}                               /* RemoveFiles */


/* SortBuffer sorts the lines in Buffer in order determined by SortTable
   using a shell sort. */
void SortBuffer(Buffer, LinePtr, LastInBuf)
char    Buffer[];               /* buffer to be sorted */
int     LastInBuf;              /* last entry in buffer */
int     LinePtr[];              /* line ptrs into Buffer */
{                               /* SortBuffer */
    int     Gap,
            I;
    register int
                    J,
                    Jg;
    int     Temp;

    for (Gap = LastInBuf / 2; (Gap > 0); Gap /= 2)
        for (I = Gap; (I < LastInBuf); I++)
            for (J = I - Gap; (J >= 0); J -= Gap) {
                Jg = J + Gap;
                if (CompareStrings(&Buffer[LinePtr[J]],
                            &Buffer[LinePtr[Jg]]) <= 0)
                    break;
                Temp = LinePtr[Jg];
                LinePtr[Jg] = LinePtr[J];
                LinePtr[J] = Temp;
            }
}                               /* SortBuffer */

/* WriteLines writes the current buffer to OutFile. */
void WriteLines(OutFile, Buffer)
FILE * OutFile;
char    Buffer[];
{                               /* WriteLines */
    int     I;

    for (I = 0; (I < NextLine); I++) {
        fputs(&Buffer[Lines[I]], OutFile);
        putc('\n', OutFile);
    }
}                               /* WriteLines */
```

29

GENPLIST and MAKPLIDX Permuted Lists and Indexes

What's a *permuted index*? It's a handy for using a set of definitions—for example, a set of C functions—where a single line describes the function's purpose and the function's name. A permuted index lets you find a function you need by looking for a word known to be inside that indexes single line.

Thus, if you set up an index so that each word appears in an alphabetized list at the beginning of a line, the task of locating the line and the function is made easier and speedier.

Study the source code (Fig. 29-1) for GENPLIST, which generates the first step in the process of ultimately developing a permuted index. Carefully note the comments contained in the code.

Then read the comments in the source code for the companion program, Fig. 29-2, which we call MAKPIDX.

To illustrate the use of a permuted index, we typed a group of sample lines of ASCII text and saved them in a file, which we call *permtest.txt* (Fig. 29-3). Assume that this text is a C program's source code. (Although it is not exactly that, its relative simplicity serves our tutorial-purpose well.)

Suppose we want to locate the function or line that contains the word "storage" or "region." Doing a line-by-line or word-by-word visual/manual search can be time-consuming, tedious, and is subject to human error. The computer can do the entire task for us quite effectively and efficiently. To do this, simulating a real situation, we will use the two programs from this chapter plus MAXSORT from Chapter 28.

Fig. 29-1. Source code for GENPLIST.

```
/* Genplist does the first step in making a permuted index. It
inserts a special symbol after each word in the input text file.
In subsequent steps in index generation, the file is sorted, and
makpidx generates the final index.

To use genplist, type

                genplist inputfile >outputfile

where inputfile is the name of the input file, and outputfile
is the name of the output file. While you may run genplist
without the outputfile (which lists output to the screen), this
intermediate file is not very useful.  */

/* Include files
 */
#include <stdio.h>
#include <ctype.h>

/* Definitions
 */
#define DASH '-'
#define ENDPRINTABLE '~'
#define EOS '\0'
#define MAXSTRLEN 255
#define STARTPRINTABLE '@'

/* Forward declarations
 */
void PermuteLine();
void OutputLine();

/* global declarations
 */
char    FoldMarker = '$';
main(argc, argv)
int     argc;
char    *argv[];
{                              /* main */
    char    InputLine[MAXSTRLEN];
    FILE * InFile = stdin;

    if (argc >= 2) {
        register int    Counter = 1;

    /* Retrieve the first command line argument. If the first character is
       a dash, this is the new FoldMarker. Verify that the character is
       OK, and if so, increment Counter. */
        if (argv[Counter][0] == DASH) {
            FoldMarker = argv[Counter][1];
            if ((FoldMarker < STARTPRINTABLE) ||
```

```
                    (FoldMarker > ENDPRINTABLE) ||
                    islower(FoldMarker)) {
                fprintf(stderr, "Invalid folding marker character.");
                exit(0);
            }
            Counter++;
        }

    /* Open the input file. */
        if ((argc >= (Counter + 1)) &&
                ((InFile = fopen(argv[Counter], "r")) == (FILE *) NULL)) {
            fprintf(stderr, "Unable to open input file.");
            exit(0);
        }
    }

 /* Read the input file line by line, and permute each line. */
    while (fgets(InputLine, MAXSTRLEN, InFile) != (char *) NULL)
        PermuteLine(InputLine);
}                               /* main */
/* PermuteLine scans through the input line character by character.
   If it finds an alphanumeric character, it writes the line starting
   from that point, and then skips the remainder of the characters
   in that sequence of alphanumeric characters. */
void PermuteLine(Line)
char   *Line;
{                               /* PermuteLine */
    register char  *InputLine;

    for (InputLine = Line;
            ((*InputLine != EOS) && (*InputLine != '\n'));
            InputLine++) {
        if (isalnum(*InputLine)) {
        /* We've got a new sequence. Write a line beginning here, and then
           skip the remainder of the sequence. */

            OutputLine(Line, InputLine);
            while (isalnum(*InputLine))
                InputLine++;
        }
    }
}                               /* PermuteLine */

/* OutputLine writes the line starting with the pointer Start, until
   it reaches the end of the line. At this point, it writes the
   FoldMarker. It then begins again with Line until it reaches Start
   again. */
void OutputLine(Line, Start)
char   *Start;
char   *Line;
{                               /* OutputLine */
    register char  *WorkingPointer;

 /* Begin with the Start pointer, and work through the string. Hitting
```

```
    either EOS or a newline stops the string. */
    for (WorkingPointer = Start;
            ((*WorkingPointer != EOS) && (*WorkingPointer != '\n'));
            WorkingPointer++)
        putchar(*WorkingPointer);
 /* Write the FoldMarker. */
    putchar(FoldMarker);

 /* Now, begin again with the beginning of the line, and write until we
    hit Start. */
    for (; (Line < Start); Line++)
        putchar(*Line);
    putchar('\n');
}                                  /* OutputLine */
```

Fig. 29-2. Source code for MAKPIDX.

```
/* Makpidx does the final transformation in making a permuted index.
Makpidx takes the output from genplist, and writes the final index.
To use makpidx, type

                makpidx inputfile [>outputfile]

where inputfile is the input file (generated from genplist), and
outputfile is the file to be created. You may run makpidx without
an outputfile. */

/* Include files
 */
#include <stdio.h>
#include <ctype.h>

/* Definitions
 */
#define DASH '-'
#define ENDPRINTABLE '~'
#define EOS '\0'
#define MAXSTRLEN 255
#define STARTPRINTABLE '@'


main(argc, argv)
int     argc;
char    *argv[];
{                                  /* main */
    char    InputLine[MAXSTRLEN];
    char    FoldMarker = '$';
    int     FoldIndex;
    extern char *strchr();
    FILE * InputFile = stdin;
    int     I,
```

```
        J;
int     Midpoint;
char    OutputLine[MAXSTRLEN];
int     OutputLength = 80;

if (argc >= 2) {
    int     Counter = 1;

/* If the first command line argument is a dash followed by any
   character other than a digit, this is the new FoldMarker to use. */
    if (argv[Counter][0] == DASH) {
        if (!isdigit(argv[Counter][1])) {
            FoldMarker = argv[Counter][1];
            if ((FoldMarker < STARTPRINTABLE)
                    || (FoldMarker > ENDPRINTABLE)
                    || islower(FoldMarker)) {
                fprintf(stderr,
                        "Invalid character %c as marker.", FoldMarker);
                exit(0);
            }
            Counter++;
        }
    }
/* If the next command line argument is a dash followed by a digit,
   this is the new OutputLength. */
    if (argv[Counter][0] == DASH) {
        if (sscanf(&argv[Counter][1], "%d", &OutputLength) != 1) {
        /* The conversion into a number failed. Abort. */

            fprintf("Unknown command line option: %s", argv[Counter]);
            exit(0);
        }

        if ((OutputLength <= 0) || (OutputLength >= (MAXSTRLEN - 1))) {
            fprintf(stderr, "Invalid output length: %d", OutputLength);
            exit(0);
        }
        Counter++;
    }
      if ((argc >= (Counter + 1)) &&
              ((InputFile = fopen(argv[Counter], "r"))
                  == (FILE *) NULL)) {
          fprintf(stderr, "Can't open file %s", argv[Counter]);
          exit(0);
      }
  }

  Midpoint = OutputLength / 2;

/* Continue reading a line at a time until we find end-of-file. */
  while (fgets(InputLine, MAXSTRLEN, InputFile) != (char *) NULL) {

  /* Blank the output line. */
```

```
    memset(OutputLine, ' ', MAXSTRLEN);

/* Find the position of the FoldMarker. */
    FoldIndex = (int) (strchr(InputLine, FoldMarker) - &InputLine[0]);

    if (FoldIndex <= 0) {    /* We've found a line with no FoldMarker.
                                This indicates a damaged input file. */
        fprintf(stderr, "The following line has no fold marker: %s",
                InputLine);
        exit(0);
    }

/* Copy all characters to the right of the FoldMarker in InputLine to
   the left hand side of OutputLine. Note that we ignore the newline
   and EOS by subtracting 2 from the input string's length. */
    J = Midpoint - 1;
    for (I = strlen(InputLine) - 2; (I > FoldIndex); I--) {
        OutputLine[J] = InputLine[I];

    /* Decrement J and wrap, if necessary. */
        J = ((J < 1) ? OutputLength - 1 : J - 1);
    }
   /* Copy all characters to the left of the foldChar in InputLine to the
      righthand side of OutputLine. */
     J = Midpoint + 1;
     for (I = 0; (I < FoldIndex); I++) {
         OutputLine[J] = InputLine[I];
     /* Increment J and wrap, if necessary. */
         J = ++J % OutputLength;
     }

   /* Find the last non-blank character in OutputLine. */
     for (J = 0; (J < OutputLength); J++)
         if (OutputLine[J] != ' ')
             I = J;

     OutputLine[++I] = '\n';
     OutputLine[++I] = EOS;
     fputs(OutputLine, stdout);
    }
}                                /* main */
```

In what will appear to be a single step, we are going to use GENPLIST to process our PERMTEST.TXT file (see the opening comments in the GENPLIST source code), MAXSORT to sort PERMTEST.TXT, and MAKPIDX to create the permuted index, which we will redirect to a new file we have arbitrarily named PERMTEST.IDX.

Ready to begin? Enter the following at the prompt on the command line:

```
genplist permtest.txt | maxsort | makpidx >permtest.idx
```

```
malloc: allocate a storage region on the heap
atof: convert ascii to floating point
atoi: convert ascii to long integer
basicget: get a record written by a basic program
bdos: execute a basic dos function
calloc: allocate an array on the heap
ceil: ceiling function
chdir: change to a new working directory
chmod: change the mode of a file
clearerr: clear a stream error
close: close a file
creat: create a new empty file
exit: terminate program execution
exp: exponential function
fabs: floating absolute value
```

Fig. 29-3. PERMTEST.TXT created for a trial run of GENPLIST.

Fig. 29-4. PERMTEST.IDX—permuted index created by MAXSORT and MAKPIDX.

```
                   bdos: execute  a basic dos function
    basicget: get a record written by  a basic program
            chmod: change the mode of  a file
                       close: close  a file
                      creat: create  a new empty file
                    chdir: change to  a new working directory
                       basicget: get  a record written by a basic program
                    malloc: allocate  a storage region on the heap
                      clearerr: clear  a stream error
                      fabs: floating  absolute value
                             malloc:  allocate a storage region on the heap
                             calloc:  allocate an array on the heap
                    calloc: allocate  an array on the heap
                 calloc: allocate an  array on the heap
                       atof: convert  ascii to floating point
                       atoi: convert  ascii to long integer
                                      atof: convert ascii to floating point
                                      atoi: convert ascii to long integer
                  bdos: execute a  basic dos function
  basicget: get a record written by a  basic program
ic program                            basicget: get a record written by a bas
                                      bdos: execute a basic dos function
    basicget: get a record written  by a basic program
                                      calloc: allocate an array on the heap
                                      ceil: ceiling function
                               ceil:  ceiling function
                              chmod:  change the mode of a file
                              chdir:  change to a new working directory
                                      chdir: change to a new working directory
```

```
fabs: floating absolute  value
 chdir: change to a new  working directory
 basicget: get a record  written by a basic program
```

and press the enter key. You can print the PERMTEST.IDX file (Fig. 29-4), which will be in ASCII. Or you can redirect the results to your printer through DOS; substitute >*prn:* for >*permtest.idx*, or to the video display by redirecting the output to >*con:*.

Either way, the end result appears in the device to which the output of MAKIPDX was redirected. Note that each word in the original file, PERMTEST.TXT, has been listed or indexed in alphabetical order to the right of the center line of the page.

APPENDICES

Appendix A
Utility Functions

The utildefn.h file, the external declaration included in the programs (*#include "utildefn.h"*) may be placed on the data disk or the compiler disk. This file describes functions that we reuse in many programs. Rather than duplicate the code for these functions in each program, we describe them in the include file, which automatically adds the actual code during the linkage process.

Our preference, when using floppy disks instead of a hard disk, is to place utildefn.h on the compiler disk and maintain the data disk exclusively for source_name.c and program_name.exe files. In this way, we never have to search for the disk with the utildefn.h file; we know it's on the disk with the compiler files. When using a hard disk we may keep the source code in a directory that is separate from the compiler; however, for speed, we may copy the course temporarily into the same directory that holds the compiler files.

Note, again, in C programming, it is *absolutely* necessary to start *all* #define and #include statements in the first column, the flush-left margin of the screen.

Using your text editor or word processor in the non-document mode with page breaks suppressed, type the lines of code exactly as shown in Fig. A-1. Carefully observe the deliberate use of upper- and lowercase letters in the code. Give the file the name UTILDEFN.H (uppercase or lowercase can be used for the file's name) and copy it onto your compiler disk or into your compiler's directory of files. No preprocessing, compiling or linking is required.

Fig. A-1. Text for UTILDEFN.H.

```
/* utildefn.h */

extern void ClearScreen() ;
extern void Prompt() ;
extern void SignOn() ;
extern void WaitASecond() ;
extern void WriteSolidLine() ;

/* utildefn.h */
```

Appendix B

Common Functions

A number of functions are used in common with most of the programs in this book. Rather than retype these functions each time source code is entered, the functions have been collected as a separate #define file named utils.c. This file must be preprocessed by the compiler to create an object file, utils.obj. When the linker is invoked as the final phase in the process of generating an executable program, this object file is linked to the object file of the program's source code.

The source for utils.c and the procedures for converting utils.c to an object file are given in this Appendix. The compilers referenced are two versions or releases of Microsoft C, one of the earliest (V1.04), a later version (v3.0), and the very latest (V4.0).

As with all C-programming source code, use your text editor or word-processor in the non-document edit mode to create the file which must be named utils.c, Fig. B-1, and place it on the same disk or directory as your compiler.

PREPROCESSING utils.c WITH MICROSOFT C COMPILER, V1.04:

Version 1.04 is actually the Lattice C compiler. Assume the disk with the compiler files is in the default drive, whatever its letter might be. From the DOS-prompt, type the following command:

```
mc1 utils<CR>
```

Fig. B-1. Source code for UTILS.C.

```
/* UTILS - COPYRIGHT 1983 by T. O. Sidebottom/L. A. Wortman  */

/*      Include Files
*/
#include <stdio.h>

/*      Definitions
*/
#define SCREENLENGTH    30
#define WAITCOUNTER     10000  /* Increase this number if delays
                                  are too short */

/* Forward declarations
*/
void ClearScreen();
void Prompt();
void SignOn();
void StripReturns();
void WaitASecond();
void WaitFiveSeconds();
void WriteSolidLine();
void WaitASecond();

/*      Supporting Routines
*/

/* ClearScreen clears the screen by writing newlines. */
void ClearScreen() {                /* ClearScreen */
    int     Count;

    for (Count = 0; Count < SCREENLENGTH; Count++)
        printf("\n");
}                                   /* ClearScreen */

/* Prompt prints Message without a newline.  It calls fflush to
   force output of the string immediately. */
void Prompt(Message)
char   *Message;
{                                   /* Prompt */
    printf("%s", Message);
    fflush(stdout);
}                                   /* Prompt */

/* SignOn prints the startup message. */
void SignOn(Message, MsgSpacing, BarLength, BarSpacing)
int     BarLength;
int     BarSpacing;
char   *Message;
int     MsgSpacing;
{                                   /* SignOn */
    int     Counter;
```

```
    ClearScreen();
    WriteSolidLine(stdout, BarLength, BarSpacing);
    printf("\n");

 /* Space over a MsgSpacing spaces before printing the Message. */
    for (Counter = 0; Counter < MsgSpacing; Counter++)
        printf(" ");
    printf("%s\n\n", Message);

    WriteSolidLine(stdout, BarLength, BarSpacing);
    WaitASecond();
    ClearScreen();
}                                   /* SignOn */

/* StripReturns removes newlines from the ends of strings. */
void StripReturns(Str)
char   *Str;
{                                   /* StripReturns */
 /* Str is a pointer to the beginning of the string. We move it until
    the character to which it points is either a '\0', indicating
    end-of-string, or a newline. */

    for (; *Str != '\0' && *Str != '\n'; Str++)
                                    /* move to end of string. */
        ;

 /* With Str properly positioned, we set the character to which it
    points to '\0'. */
    *Str = '\0';
}                                   /* StripReturns */

/* WaitASecond pauses for a second by using a wait loop. */
void WaitASecond() {                /* WaitASecond */
    long    Count;

    for (Count = 0; Count < WAITCOUNTER; Count++);
}                                   /* WaitASecond */

/* WaitFiveSeconds pauses for five seconds by calling WaitASecond
   five times. */
void WaitFiveSeconds() {          /* WaitFiveSeconds */
    int     Counter;

    for (Counter = 0; Counter < 5; Counter++)
        WaitASecond();
}                                   /* WaitFiveSeconds */

/* WriteSolidLine first prints a series of characters to properly
   indent the solid line, and then prints a sequence of stars. */
void WriteSolidLine(OutFile, Length, Spacing)
FILE * OutFile;
int     Length;
int     Spacing;
{                                   /* WriteSolidLine */
```

```
    int     Counter;

    for (Counter = 0; Counter < Spacing; Counter++)
        fprintf(OutFile, " ");
    for (Counter = 0; Counter < Length; Counter++)
        fprintf(OutFile, "*");
    fprintf(OutFile, "\n");
}                               /* WriteSolidLine */
```

When the DOS-prompt reappears, type this command:

mc2 utils<CR>

When the DOS-prompt reappears, call up the disk's directory with the DIR command. You will find that, in addition to utils.c, the file named "utils.obj" is now on the disk.

Once the utils.obj file has been created, the source code utils.c will not be used at all to process the programs in this book. However, the utils.c file may be stored on the disk for later use or for introducing your own revisions. If the source code is revised at any time, it must be preprocessed as above to generate a new object file.

PREPROCESSING utils.c FOR THE MICROSOFT C COMPILER, V3.0 and V4.0:

This is the version of the Microsoft C-compiler introduced in July 1986. It is an update of Microsoft's Version 3.0, which is proprietary to Microsoft and, to be expected, is called up a bit differently. Version 3.0 is a four-pass and Version 4.0 is a three-pass compiler, with code optimizers. The passes can be called with a single command:

msc source_name;<CR>

Do not omit the semicolon after source_name. The msc command generates the object file. Thus if the source_name is utils, the object file utils.obj is generated.

Complete batch files for compiling and linking are given in Appendix C.

Appendix C
Compiler Notes

The number of commercially available compilers for the C programming language is rapidly increasing. Although most claim to follow the syntax created by Kernighan and Ritchie (and often referred to as the "de facto standard"), each of the compilers may be supplied with a run-time library that is different from the other compilers. These differences can result in variations or departures from the "de facto standard," which may mean source code successfully compiled and executed on one compiler may not be as successful with another compiler—despite the creators' claims to compatibility.

Programmers, too, tend to develop favorites among the compilers with which they have had the opportunity to work. Although we are users rather than creators of compilers, we do have our favorite. Our preference is based on: similarity to (or, relative compatibility with) the UNIX library; speed of compilation; compactness of the code it generates in the executable form; and speed with which the compiled code is executed. One does have to make a choice. We've unambiguously declared our preference.

Note, too, some compilers are designed to "optimize" sections of the source code during the compilation process. This does not release the programmer from the responsibility of writing code that is tight or efficient.

The compiler that has been used to test the syntax and accuracy of the code in this book is Microsoft C, Version 4.0, published by the Microsoft Corporation, Redmond, Washington.

Other compilers may work with the source code in this book, as is, or with necessary changes in syntax. However, we know the compiler referred to in this book does work, and works very well. The code was created, compiled, linked and tested with the IBM PC, XT, and an 8MHz AT. If you have a compiler different from the one we selected, do check the documentation and make any syntactical changes that may be indicated. Begin by trying your compiler with the source code as published in this book. Pay special attention to any error messages the compiler may generate. A well-designed compiler liberally gives clues to possible errors in the source code. Some of the programs in this book may work without requiring changes. Try them first as they are before attempting changes.

The source code for utildefn.h, which is used in most of the programs in this book, is in Appendix A and can be transferred without preprocessing to the disk on which your compiler's files are stored. The source code from which utils.obj is created is in Appendix B, with instructions on how to generate the object file.

The following paragraphs are intended purely as a guide to how to create a batch file for preprocessing, parsing, generating machine code, optimizing, and linking source code. A different compiler publisher may change the procedure for calling the various phases of the compiler and linker. Check the documentation for the release version of your compiler-linker to determine and implement any revisions to the batch file that may be required. We include batch files for the Microsoft C, Version 3.0, 4.0, and the earlier Version 1.04.

BATCH FILE FOR MICROSOFT C, VERSIONS 3.0 AND 4.0

The batch file we use for Microsoft C, Versions 3.0 and 4.0 automatically links the source code with the compiler's floating point library and the object file utils. Of course, you should name the file to suit your own style. We call it GO.BAT. Figure C-1 is the text for the batch file we used with the IBM AT and the source code contained in this book.

BATCH FILE FOR MICROSOFT C, VERSION 1.04

Figure C-2 is the text of the batch file for Version 1.04. Note that in both batch files the two files, source_name.map and source_name.obj, which are generated during the compiling/linking process, are automatically erased by the relevant lines *erase %1.map* and *erase %1.obj*.

To run either batch file, assuming you've named them GO.BAT, at the DOS-prompt or command line, enter:

```
GO source_name
```

In versions 3.0 and 4.0 the compiler's three or four passes are automatically sequenced with the *msc %1;* command. Version 1.04 makes two passes, mc1 and mc2. If the compilation succeeds, the batch file calls the linker and the appropriate floating-point library. If this phase succeeds, the compiler-linker should have produced a file named source_name.EXE. This file should be executable. As a quick test, it is automatically executed when the go.bat batch

```
echo off
cls
echo Compile:  %1.C (with floating point support)
echo Link to:  UTILS.OBJ
echo .
echo .
msc %1;
echo off
if errorlevel 1 goto bleep
echo .
echo . link %1+UTILS,,,slibfp;
link %1+UTILS,,,slibfp;
echo .
echo off
if errorlevel 1 goto bleep
echo .
erase %1.map
erase %1.obj
:bleep
BEEP
end
%1
```

Fig. C-1. Batch file for Microsoft compilers V3.0 and V4.0.

```
mc1 %1
mc2 %1
link C %1 UTILS,%1,,MC.LIB
erase %1.map
erase %1.obj
%1
```

Fig. C-2. Batch file for the early Microsoft compiler V1.04.

file recognizes the last line in the file, %1, which is the completed source_name program.

Special note: if during the linking phase while you are compiling TDVAR and you are using the Microsoft Version 4.0 compiler you see the message *ERROR 2000 STACK OVERFLOW,* add the optional ST switch to the linker as follows (assuming TDVAR is the name of the file being compiled and linked):

```
>LINK /ST:4000 TDVAR +UTILS, , ,SLIBFP;
```

Note, too, the *if errorlevel 1* traps in the batch file. The procedure is aborted automatically by the batch file if an *error,* not a *warning,* is detected during any of the compiler's passes or during the link phase.

Enjoy!

Index

Index